THE
CONTINUAL
INNER
SEARCH

Roy and the author 1955

MARGARET WINN is the daughter of Roy's first son, Dick, who raised her to follow Roy's approach to life. Although she spent most of her childhood with her mother's side of the family, the gregarious Parkes', she always felt more Winn than Parkes. She has a background in anthropology and education. Her professional life has been spent in Asia, Africa and the Pacific working on sexual and reproductive health aid and development projects.

THE CONTINUAL INNER SEARCH
The Life of Roy Winn

MARGARET WINN

KERR
Melbourne, Victoria

First published 2020
Kerr Publishing Pty Ltd
Melbourne, Victoria
ABN 64 124 219 638

© 2020 Margaret Winn

This book is copyright. Apart from fair dealing for the purpose of private study, research, criticism or review, or under Copyright Agency Ltd rules of recording, no part may be reproduced by any means.
The moral right of the author has been asserted.

ISBN 978-1-875703-28-9 (eBook)
ISBN 978-1-875703-29-6 (Print on Demand, PoD)

BIC Category:	Biography & Autobiography
BISAC Category 1:	BIO017000 BIOGRAPHY & AUTOBIOGRAPHY/Medical
BISAC Category 2:	BIO008000 BIOGRAPHY & AUTOBIOGRAPHY/Military
BISAC Category 3:	HIS004000/Australia & New Zealand

Cover photograph: Roy Winn c.1943
Cover and book design: Paul Taylder of Xigrafix Media & Design
Photographs and illustrations supplied by Margaret Winn, unless otherwise noted
Typeset in Adobe Caslon Pro 11/15pt

Print-on-Demand and eBook distribution: ebookalchemy.com.au

National Library of Australia PrePublication Data Service:

 A catalogue record for this book is available from the National Library of Australia

*To my Winn family and all those who, like Roy,
live their lives according to their own code*

Of Roy Winn:
    ... dedicated to the continual inner search to understand himself and others

Janet Nield, 1974

Contents

	Introduction	1
1	A Privileged Upbringing	7
2	Off to War – Gallipoli and Egypt	19
3	The Western Front takes its toll	45
4	The Catalyst for the Inner Search	77
5	Psychoanalytical Treatment in the UK	83
6	Committing to the Inner Search	89
7	Family Life	111
8	Poems and Nonsense Verse	131
9	Last Words	141
	Appendix 1	148
	Winn Family Tree	
	Appendix 2	151
	William Winn and a Short History of Winn's Limited	
	Acknowledgements	165
	Indexes	168

THE CONTINUAL INNER SEARCH

Roy c.1943

Introduction

I have wanted to write about Roy Winn's life for many years. Roy was my grandfather and very close to my father Dick, his elder son, although I did not know him well. I was only 11 when he died.

Roy was Australia's first full-time practising psychoanalyst, a career born out of his personal experiences during the First World War. He spent a lifetime exploring the mind, trying to understand himself and others.

My father thought very highly of him, believing Roy to be an original thinker and a man of integrity who lived his own life according to his own code, seemingly unswayed by the prevailing moral climate or conventional social niceties. In Roy's own writings, he reveals himself as witty and self-mocking, insightful and inventive. His colleagues in psychoanalysis saw him as kindly and tolerant, a man of great personal charm and fine character who had a ready smile for the foibles of human nature and acute insight into unconscious mental processes.[1] He was said to have had a keen sense of humour.[2]

And yet I never felt entirely comfortable with Roy. I found him reserved and disengaged, uninterested in getting to know me. He did not seem to bother with idle chitchat and only spoke if he considered there was something worthwhile to say, although if you asked him a question he was pleased to answer. He was a chain-smoker, lighting

---

1   Graham F *Obituary of Roy Coupland Winn* MJA February 1964 p333
2   Garton S *Australian Dictionary of Biography* ANU Vol. 12 1990

a fresh cigarette from his previous one, which left him with yellow nicotine stains that, as a child, I found repellent. His wooden leg both fascinated and embarrassed me.

Nevertheless, even then, I knew him to be something special, someone to be remembered.

My mother Helen's side of the family included many larger than life characters who were actively remembered. Helen was the grand-daughter of Sir Henry Parkes, the Father of Federation, and the daughter of Cobden Parkes, the Government Architect. Her house was full of Parkes' heirlooms and memorabilia. She was connected to the wider Parkes clan and told Parkes' family stories until we knew them by heart. In her sitting-room was an enormous marble bust with an imposing bosom and imperious gaze. It was of Eleanor, Sir Henry's second wife. In the same way that Eleanor dominated that sitting room, so the Parkes family dominated the historical record of our family. We knew very little about the Winn side of my family and I liked the idea of redressing the balance.

There are many biographical details about Roy in various psychoanalytical histories and First World War books but I thought his descendants deserved a fuller picture. All those who knew Roy well – his brothers, two wives, Nanny, children and friends – are now dead, but I had videotaped interviews of my father Dick, my uncle and aunt Murray and Evelyne Winn, and their first cousin Janet Winn, and I expected that these tapes would provide a good picture of what Roy was really like and how he thought, rather than just what he did.

Despite long sessions over a number of days and notwithstanding their ability to recall specific incidents and activities, these interviews, frustratingly, provided little insight into his character, thinking or motivations. This should not have surprised me: most of the Winns I have known have tilted towards science and technology rather than the humanities, the rational rather than the emotional, the concrete rather than the speculative. Roy's family could easily remember Winn telephone numbers and car registration plates, but could not so easily reflect on the nuances of Roy's personality.

I turned to Roy's two small diaries of the war and immediate post-war years, but there is not a lot to be learned from them except chronology and the scope of his activity. Roy's Gallipoli photograph album, as well as his poems, nonsense verse and medical musings provide texture but the big hole in all the available material was in understanding his psyche. Given his work as a pioneering doctor of the mind in Australia, it was a hole I felt I needed to fill.

A handwritten document titled *Men May Rise*, which was found in Roy's papers after his death, proved to be a treasure trove. It is an undated, unpublished novel written under the pseudonym John Truscott. All three of Roy's children considered the novel to be largely autobiographical. My uncle Murray had typed copies made for family members in the late 1990s, which was fortunate, as the original manuscript has subsequently disappeared.

Besides information about Roy's involvement in the war, *Men May Rise* provided insights into Roy's thoughts and feelings about this momentous time in his life – and in world history. It tells the story of a young man, Tas Selton, who leaves Australia with the Australian Army Medical Corps and is posted to Gallipoli in 1915. The young Tas had originally intended to become a medical missionary but, as he progressed through medical school, he came to doubt his suitability for that particular calling. The novel focuses on Tas's war service and courtship, the severe depression and jealousy that followed and his successful psychoanalytical treatment. Tas comes across as a real person and the descriptions of war have the ring of authenticity, although the supporting characters from the love story are somewhat one-dimensional and the dialogue is wooden and stilted.

Roy was no novelist but, like my father, aunt and uncle, I believe its real value lies in its realism – a faithful rendering of Roy's own lived experience from 1915 until about 1923. This view is reinforced by the author's note which says 'this novel may seem rather more biographical than customary… there is no character in this book who has not, so the author hopes, a faint resemblance to some living person.'[3]

I suspect that Roy wrote the novel as part of a conscious therapeutic process, believing that recovery was assisted by reflecting on a traumatic experience through writing or talking about it. Given that the accounts of particular battles accurately mimic what we know of Roy's actual war experience, one cannot help but speculate that Tas was Roy's alter ego and that putting pen to paper likely was designed to help Roy exorcise some of his war-inflicted demons. Rather than laboriously using endless quotation marks, I have chosen to insert some of the novel's text directly into this biography and have substituted 'Roy' for 'Tas' so that the excerpts from the novel appear as part of the narrative. I cannot be certain that every passage used in this way is an accurate record of what Roy did or what happened during this period, but it is clear that, even if it is not, it is as close to a first-hand account of the events described as one could hope. Although this decision could result in a less than fully accurate history, it is a price I decided to pay in order to flesh out Roy's emotional state, about which we otherwise would be ignorant.

With regard to the text, Roy's spelling is sometimes idiosyncratic. Rather than attempt to correct or highlight everything with a *sic*, I have generally left his words as he wrote and spelt them. Similarly, I have left measurements in acres, feet and yards as I found them.

All the photographs used in the book are from Winn archives, except the one of Winn houses on Mayfield Ridge which is from the University of Newcastle. The Gallipoli photographs were taken by Roy in 1915 and, although their quality is variable, they demonstrate the subjects that Roy found worth recording at the time.

Several generations of Winns covered in this biography anointed their descendants with a limited range of given names, such as William, Janet and Betty, and then proceeded to use them or similar names, as nicknames for other members of the clan. This practice could have

---

[3] Winn RC *Men May Rise* p1

caused significant confusion, so I have consistently used given names, rather than nicknames. Hence the name Bertha is used for Roy's wife, even though he always called her 'Betty'; and his daughter Betty is referred to as 'Betty', even though Roy's pet names for her were 'Bettina' or 'Bonnie'. The only exceptions are Roy's oldest brother, William Harold Winn, who everyone referred to as 'Harold', his wife Ellie McMurtrie and my father Dick.

I have copies of Roy's main professional publications and some of his medical, philosophical and poetic writings, but privacy and confidentiality concerns meant I did not have access to patient case notes or sensitive material held at the various psychoanalytical institutes. The sum of all the available material relating to Roy is scant and occasionally contradictory[4] and I suspect the inevitable paucity of personal and professional biographical material will raise questions that I will never be able to answer. Still, I think it is worth doing what I can in order to present this most singular of men to his descendants.

---

[4] Official records have conflicting dates and details

THE CONTINUAL INNER SEARCH

Roy as a child

I

A Privileged Upbringing

Roy Coupland Winn was born on 26 June 1890 into a God-fearing family which was on the rise socially and materially. His parents were William and Janet Winn[5] *née* Shade. They already had three sons. Roy was to be their last child.

Roy's birth certificate lists his residence as North Waratah, which at that time was part of Mayfield on the outskirts of Newcastle, an area where the well-to-do were buying acreages and building grand homes. During his early years, it is likely his parents were living at Winnonaville, a substantial Victorian house on two acres of land at 15 Kerr Street, and later at Winn Court, a larger Victorian house with wide verandahs and five acres of land on the ridge overlooking paddocks leading down to the Hunter River.

Roy was given Coupland as his middle name as a nod to Harriet, his grandmother on his father's side who, before her marriage to John Winn[6] had been a Coupland from Lincolnshire. Roy described his grandmother Harriet as 'a Personality'.[7] Whenever Harriet came to visit, she would never walk up the path from the front gate, she would gallop. Despite the alcoholism and early death of her husband, Harriet had been instrumental in holding her family together and, from the 1850s, in successfully establishing the first of the many Winn's drapery stores in Newcastle.

---

5   Janet Winn was known as Jessie
6   John was also known as James or Isaac Winn
7   Winn RC *Fragment of a letter* unaddressed, undated

William and Janet Winn

Roy's father William[8] was listed on his birth certificate as a draper aged 41. He called himself 'a merchant' but is better described as a canny and energetic businessman with determination and practical ability. With his brother Isaac, he further developed drapery businesses in Newcastle and then moved south to establish and run various enterprises in Sydney. During his time at the helm, Winn's Ltd was a very successful conglomerate. William was well connected to the movers and shakers of the Sydney Establishment and was regularly cited in newspapers as a well-known figure in the business communities of Newcastle and Sydney.

For sport, William shot targets and won a number of prizes. He was prone to losing his temper when people were foolish but would make an apology afterwards.[9] He had a short beard that pricked his grandchildren's faces when he kissed them.

---

8   William Winn 1849-1929
9   Winn RC *Letter to Betty* 20 February 1961

Roy (left), Gordon, Janet, William, Ellie McMurtrie, Harold, Stanley

A staunch Methodist, William set great store by integrity and uprightness and was vehemently against the consumption of alcohol. Vice president of the New South Wales Temperance Alliance, newspapers occasionally referred to him as 'Wowser Winn'.[10] His uncompromising temperance stand may have been reinforced by the alcoholism of his father John, who reportedly fell from his horse when drunk, damaged his skull and eventually died in 1855, aged only 40, suffering such severe mental problems that people thought he had gone mad.[11]

William had positions of responsibility in Methodist church affairs in Newcastle and later in Sydney. The Winns funded the building of the Mayfield Methodist Church and there is still a Winn Hall in its grounds. William, together with his great friend William Arnott of biscuit company fame, chartered space on a ship to bring New

---

10 Winn RW *Memoirs of Richard (Dick) Winn* 2003 p5
11 *Death certificate* of John Winn who was buried at the Field of Mars Cemetery, Sydney

Bush picnic: Roy (middle row, right) with striped tie

Testaments from England to Sydney in order to spread the gospel. The Winns and the Arnotts maintained a close familial friendship which lasted for three generations.

At William's funeral in 1929, there were many notables from the Methodist church hierarchy, the YMCA, Salvation Army, as well as a large representation of Winn's Ltd staff. In his will, William left £200 to the Methodist Foreign Missionary Society and £200 to the British and Foreign Bible Society – not inconsiderable amounts in 1929. William is buried in the Methodist section of Rookwood Cemetery near his mother Harriet.

Janet's parents were Thomas Shade and Sophia Cameron, who was part of the big Donald Cameron clan centred on Stroud in NSW. Janet[12] shared William's Methodism. According to Roy she had the countenance of a saint, religious emotion was the joy of life itself and the Sermon on the Mount a literal guide for how she conducted herself.[13] She was a little dour, believed in self-denial and tried to make others

---

12   Janet Winn 1845-1938
13   Winn RC *Men May Rise* p3

Camping with brothers: Roy (second left)

do the same.[14] She was quiet and in later life always dressed in black.[15]

William and Janet had three sons before Roy. The first was William Harold, born in 1883 and always known as Harold. He was eventually the director of Winn's Ltd in Newcastle. In February 1917, he married Helen (Ellie) McMurtrie from Braeside at Lady Martins Beach, Wolseley Road, Point Piper. They had a daughter, Janet Winn, a widely respected dietitian.[16] Harold died at 64 in 1948.

The second son was Gordon Russell, born in 1887. He married Ellie's sister, Ida McMurtrie, in November 1916 and became managing director of Winn's Ltd in Sydney. They had a daughter Nora and a baby boy who died young. Their granddaughter is Pru Brewer.

The third son was Stanley Dickson, who was born in 1889. Born deaf, it is likely that Stanley was schooled at the New South Wales Institution for the Deaf, Dumb and Blind established in 1872, the first

---

14 Winn RC *Men May Rise* p47
15 Winn Murray *personal communication* 2008
16 Harold Winn's daughter, Janet Winn, should not be confused with her grandmother, Janet (Jessie) Winn

school and boarding facility for the deaf in Australia. Family lore has it that William supported the institution financially. Stanley could deaf sign but lip-reading was the main method of communication within the family. Stanley married Henrietta (Isabel) Arrell who was not deaf when she met Stanley but became so after an illness. She and Stanley had six children – Stanley, Harry, Edena, Reta, Annesley who was also deaf, and Rodney. Over time, Stan's family participated less and less often at large family gatherings, probably because of the communication difficulties encountered with large groups.[17] Stanley died at 59 after being hit by a car.

Roy was born a year after Stanley. William and Janet also had two other children who died at birth – a sister Jessie Harriet in 1879 and an unnamed boy in 1881, two years before Harold.

In the 1890s, as William moved between businesses in Sydney and Newcastle, he bought himself a mansion in Sydney's inner west at Concord, possibly in Davidson Ave, with a four-acre orchard set in 20 acres of pasture. This was sold after five years as he needed to return to Newcastle to repair the business that Isaac had been running there, but with less success than was anticipated.

Once William was satisfied he could leave the Newcastle business in the more capable hands of Isaac's son, also called William, he focused on developing Winn's Ltd in Sydney and he bought Rockley, a large, gracious, turn-of-the-century house in what was then called Campbell Street on Milsons Point.[18] It had extensive views across Sydney Harbour to Garden Island, Circular Quay and the Rocks. The family used the ferries that eventually brought cars between the south and north shores of the harbour.

My father Dick remembered the Milsons Point house well. To his childhood eye, the lounge room was full of marvels brought back from various Winn trips overseas. There were black carved dragon tables

---

17 Winn Janet *personal communication* 2008
18 Address is now Upper Pitt St, Kirribilli

Rockley c.1910

and huge Chinese vases, which Dick remembered as being taller than he was and like something out of *Ali Baba and the Forty Thieves*. There were prizes from William's target shooting successes, including a fancy clock on the mantlepiece.

My Uncle Murray's memories of the house were different. He remembered a big woodpile on the east side of the house, an attic from which children were excluded and an ever-present widowed grandmother.[19]

All of Roy's children remember assembling at the house for a family lunch every Saturday. A full-time cook and housekeeper regularly produced roast chicken, considered a great delicacy. Betty recalled hot plum pudding and cream desserts.[20] The only sour note from Dick's point of view was the cutlery. The knife handles were of ivory which went brown and shrank with a lot of washing. This resulted in a space opening up between the handle and the blade, which would fill up with a greyish deposit that revolted him.[21]

William would go down on one knee to say the Grace: 'For what we are about to receive may the Lord make us truly grateful. Amen.'[22] Dick and Murray's cousin, Janet, remembers that the saying of grace preceded all meals and that prayers were recited after breakfast on Christmas Day, further delaying the giving of presents. Rockley Christmases, she recalls, were not nearly as much fun as those at Point Piper where her McMurtrie grandmother lived.[23]

I have no information about Roy's early schooling. In January 1906, aged 15, he started at Sydney Grammar School in College Street in the city, finishing there in December 1909. The school's archivist could provide little information about Roy's time at the school, apart from the fact that, after the First World War, he contributed £10 for the school's war memorial. I know Roy won the Class 4 Greek prize in 1907 and received a copy of Homer's *Odyssey* because that is written on the book's flyleaf. It was an appropriate award as, throughout his life, Roy maintained a keen interest in classical literature.

Roy's two older brothers, Harold and Gordon, had gone to the bastion of Methodist education, Newington in Stanmore, but there

---

19 Winn Murray *personal communication* 2008
20 Ferguson Betty *Recollections of Sydney Harbour before the Bridge* undated
21 Winn RW *Memoirs of Richard (Dick) Winn* 2003 p13
22 Ferguson Betty *Recollections of Sydney Harbour before the Bridge* undated
23 Winn Janet *personal communication* 2008

A Privileged Upbringing

Sydney Grammar School: Roy (middle row right)

is no record of Roy ever attending the school. One can only speculate why Roy wasn't enrolled. Dick maintained that the strict religious teachings of Newington would not have suited atheist Roy, that the non-denominational Sydney Grammar School would have been more to his taste. This may well have been true but it flies in the face of Roy's apparent personal piety as well as his pious upbringing. Dick wrote: 'His mother wanted him to be a Methodist missionary and when he was seven years old he was taken to stand in church and swear he would never drink alcohol.'[24]

William and Janet initially had wanted Harold to be a missionary but having come dux of Newington he became interested in teaching as a profession. His parents would not support an alternative career like one in education, so Harold went into the family business instead.[25] As Gordon was less academically able and Stanley was deaf, William and

---

24 Winn RW *Memoirs of Richard (Dick) Winn* 2003 p5
25 Winn Janet *personal communication* 2008

Sydney University Medicine: Roy (back row, middle)

Janet appear to have turned their sights on Roy to fulfill their desire for a missionary son.

After completing school, Roy went straight to Sydney University to commence a medical degree. It was 1910 and his initial idea was that on graduation he would go to the South Sea Islands as a medical missionary. According to *Men May Rise*, he initially fixed on being an ordinary missionary, but later decided he would not do any preaching work at all.[26] The philosophical and belief processes involved in this slippage from preaching missionary to medical missionary are unclear, but Roy eventually lost all belief in God, even though he never lost his desire to be of help to others.

---

26   Winn RC *Men May Rise* p48

Roy gained a number of honours in the various medical examinations.[27] He graduated bachelor of medicine and master of surgery in 1915. He was appointed Junior Resident Medical Officer at Royal Prince Alfred Hospital, Sydney.

Photos of Roy during these years show an attractive man, five feet eight inches tall, with black hair, hazel eyes and a piercing gaze. His passport describes him as having a broad forehead, ordinary face, straight nose, round chin and dark complexion.[28] He was part of a close-knit family of sons who were integrated into a wider familial network of successful Winn businesses, with all members leading socially conventional lives. The expectation was of a life of comfort, status and privilege, in return for upright and honorable service under the umbrella of a robust conservative Methodism.

Roy c.1910

---

27   Sydney Grammar School Issue 213 *Sydneian* September 1912
28   Passport issued by UK Foreign Office 8 April 1918

Captain Roy Winn in uniform

2

Off to War – Gallipoli and Egypt

In July 1915, before he had finished his hospital residency, Roy signed up for what came to be called the First World War. He volunteered out of a sense of duty – he felt he simply had to go. He sympathised with conscientious objectors and doubted whether, if he had not been a doctor, he would have enlisted, as he could not have taken on the killing.[29] Not only did he have to overcome his own reluctance to enlist, there were other matters to consider before deciding. The Medical Superintendent of Royal Prince Alfred Hospital told Roy that he did not want him to go and if he did, he would make it hard for Roy to get a job after the war.[30] At this time, the Sydney medical fraternity was small and interconnected, so any threats to his future medical career had to be taken seriously.

Roy volunteered anyway and was commissioned captain in the Australian Medical Corps. He was assigned to the No. 1 Australian General Hospital, in the enormous former Heliopolis Palace Hotel, Cairo. He had sailed with 20 other doctors and 100 nurses on the mail steamer *Orontes* and arrived in Egypt on 3 September 1915. When he undertook his first ward rounds, he was pleased to find that the men under his care were all suffering from medical complaints; he did not

---

29   Winn RC *Men May Rise* p48
30   Winn Dick *personal communication* 2002

yet regard himself as competent to handle wounded surgical patients.[31]

When on leave he explored Cairo. He went to the antiquities museum and was 'overwhelmed by the magnificence and gorgeous colouring of the furniture and the jewellery used so many thousands

---

31   Winn RC *Men May Rise* p17

of years ago. He was impressed by the forceful representation of a court official known as Sheik-el-Beled because it was not too conventional.'[32] Although Roy had a strict religious upbringing and seemed to be very conformist, this suggests he was not blind to the attractions of the unconventional.

He also sampled the Cairo nightlife with fellow medical officers, including one trip to a 'can-can' cabaret. He viewed the cabaret as a debased form of folk dance, which might have been appropriate when performed by village maidens as a prelude to courtship.[33] This comment of Roy's is in keeping with the strain of prudishness and naiveté that runs through his novel.

He went to the Casino de Paris for a more conventional cabaret. The dancers sat at tables with the patrons and one girl challenged him *'vous êtes vierge, Monsigneur le Capitan, n'est pas?'* He felt embarrassed and tried not to show it but the wound to his vanity persisted for some time.[34] One can speculate whether Roy acted to prevent a repeat of this humiliating experience or whether his religious beliefs forbade it.

In the face of lack of progress against Germany in 1914, the British War Council had decided to attack Germany's weaker allies and a plan was devised to capture the Turkish forts commanding the narrow Dardanelles and force open a way to Istanbul. After naval attempts proved unsuccessful, a land attack was approved and, in April 1915, British and Anzac formations landed at Cape Helles and Anzac Cove, both part of the Turkish peninsula that the Turks called Gelibolu. The terrain was precipitous and heavily defended and although both sides fought bravely, after some early gains the troops remained deadlocked in static trench warfare. On the first day, more than 620 Australians died, a shock to Australians who had come together in a Commonwealth just 14 years before.

---

32 Winn RC *Men May Rise* p19
33 Winn RC *Men May Rise* p20
34 Winn RC *Men May Rise* p20

Cropped hair

Rather than stay in Egypt, Roy decided to volunteer for service on Gallipoli and on 27 September 1915 he left Cairo on a hospital ship bound for Mudros Harbour on the island of Lemnos. En route, the party had their hair cropped and he was amazed by the transformation from respectable individuals into undoubted criminals.[35]

At Mudros he was transferred at dusk to an ex-Channel steamer for the last leg to Gallipoli. The sound of distant shelling could be heard, with sudden flashes and bright arcs of searchlights. He describes it as like a monster fireworks display. The brilliant beams lit up circles of hillside as if it were day and exposed perfect targets, and bursting shells caused fantastic columns of dust-laden smoke to swirl upward like volcanic eruptions.[36]

The crack of rifle fire and the sputter of machineguns was almost continuous at times, while the loud boom of artillery and the roar of bursting shells acted as a bass accompaniment to the staccato treble. At other periods, only occasional shots would be heard, so the effect was of swelling storms of sound alternating with quietness. It resembled nothing so much as the movements of a soul-stirring symphony played by a mighty orchestra. Roy felt as though his heart would break.[37] Although this description of the approach to Gallipoli is taken from his novel, it illustrates that Roy was a man with imagination and a poetic bent.

---

35   Winn RC *Men May Rise* p26
36   Winn RC *Men May Rise* p27
37   Winn RC *Men May Rise* p27

Above: Anzac Cove pier *Below:* Anzac Cove ordnance stores

The party was put into ship's boats, which were towed by pinnaces towards the Gallipoli shore in the dark. As they approached Anzac Cove, Roy could hear the frightening zip of bullets striking the water around him. He hoped that all would find such a harmless target. He felt proud he was about to step onto that heroic shore, but thought how differently he was faring from those who had scaled the cliffs in the light of dawn only a few months before.

The boats drew alongside a small pier and he clambered out, careful not to blunder into ammunition boxes, shells, cases of bully beef, jam tins and rolls of barbed wire. The party of medicos was eventually conducted to the dugout of the director of medical services, who announced 'just as well you've come. We're needing you badly.'[38] They were accommodated in a kind of blockhouse with walls of bully beef cases and a tarpaulin roof. Roy slept badly.

Main sap to Fisherman's Hut with Maori tiki

Next day he reported for duty to the 1st Light Horse Field Ambulance at Fisherman's Hut. The ambulance station was partly sheltered by low hills between the Turkish lines and Fisherman's Beach. There was only one medical officer there, where once there had been a complement of six. Although there had not been much fighting since the last battle in August, many soldiers had dysentery and those that recovered usually managed to acquire paratyphoid or jaundice.[39]

---

38 Winn RC *Men May Rise* p27
39 Winn RC *Men May Rise* p28

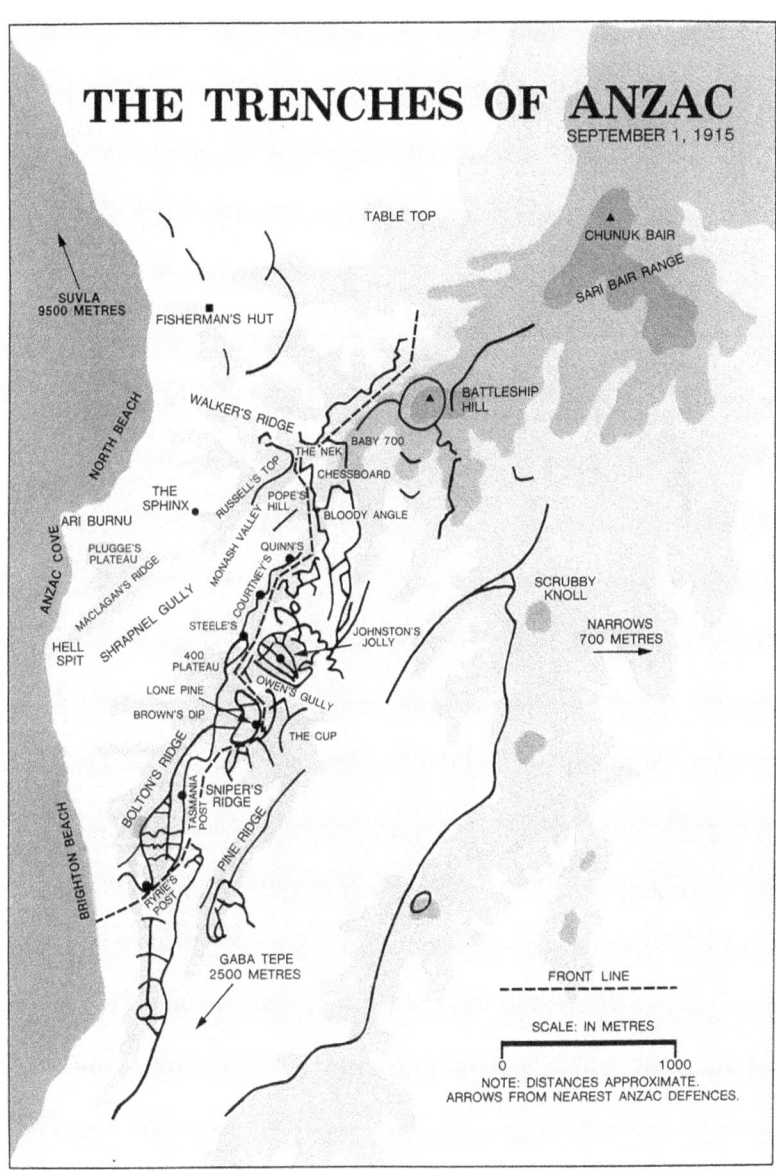

Illustration from *Gallipoli The Incredible Campaign*

The newcomers were each assigned a batman who assisted in the preparation of a dugout for his nominal master. The preferred sites were on the side of a hill with the only proviso of importance being a

Sharpening bayonets

site facing the opposite way to the enemy. Roy's dugout was made of a wooden plank and pilfered rubber sheets to keep out the rain. It was constructed without mishap on a second site, after his batman pointed out that the initial choice was exposed to shellfire.[40]

Two weeks passed and Roy was surprised to find himself still alive, if somewhat jumpy. The Turks did not appear to be interested in him and, in addition, as far as Roy was concerned, they had demonstrated their inability to hit a moving target. For his part, he sincerely hoped that if he were to become a target at all, he would always remain a moving one. Meanwhile, he was still able to number himself among the quick – extremely quick at times so he considered – and was almost beginning to enjoy himself. He had never been to a race meeting in his life but wondered whether a horse race would prove rather tame without an occasional burst of shrapnel to spur on the contestants![41]

One amusement was bathing. It was not as enjoyable as surfing on the beaches of Sydney, not only because there was no surf but because Johnnie Turk persisted in shelling the beach at unscheduled times.

---

40 Winn RC *Men May Rise* p28
41 Winn RC *Men May Rise* p30

There was a compensation for this drawback in the fact that the wearing of costumes was not compulsory.[42] It appears from these wry passages that humour was one method Roy used to handle his fears.

Less than three weeks after his arrival at Anzac, Roy received instructions that he had been transferred to 14th Infantry Battalion of the 4th Brigade, which was in a rest camp at Mudros. He left Gallipoli on 22 October 1915, for Lemnos where he was to replace the sick Henry Loughran as Regimental Medical Officer, RMO. Away from the fighting, the health of the troops improved but their numbers were at half strength until a large number of reinforcements joined the units soon after Roy arrived. Roy took longer to fit into his new environment than other colleagues he knew, but he slowly began to make new friends.[43]

Roy returned to Gallipoli on 1 November 1915. The brigade was marched to a gully north of Fisherman's Hut. The Australian dugouts were excavated on the coastal side of the ridge and protected from direct fire. Roy used his surgical bag as a pillow. He felt that, despite its knobbiness, laying hands on it might be easier if it was never out of reach. This action became a habit. The bag never left his side by day and it took the place of his huge revolver.[44] Dick always maintained that Roy refused to wear his pistol as he was not planning on killing anyone and needed more space on his belt for bandages.[45]

On Roy's first night, he slept fitfully owing to the attentions of what he thought was a flea but which, on inspection, turned out to be a louse. He got the horrors, tore off all his clothes and soaked them in Lysol. After he put on clean underclothes, he immediately excavated a new dugout. After several days, he was pleased to see that his methods had proved effective.[46]

---

42   Winn RC *Men May Rise* p30
43   Winn RC *Men May Rise* p30
44   Winn RC *Men May Rise* p59
45   Winn Dick *personal communication* 2003
46   Winn RC *Men May Rise* p60

The brigade was told to occupy the Turkish trenches which had been taken six weeks previously. The frontline trenches formed a salient, bulging into enemy territory, opposite a mountainous hilltop known as 971. The hill was still in Turkish hands despite the loss of many lives during the August battle.[47]

The trenches the Australians were using were overlooked by the enemy and exposed to stray bullets coming from the flank. These had travelled a long distance and lost considerable momentum. They made a whistling sound and were called 'canaries'. At times the canaries were silent, at other times they were so numerous that their passing sounded like summer showers, stinging the parched soil.[48]

Stray bullets were not the only pests encountered on Gallipoli. Flies hummed with even greater persistence than the bullets, and lice were far from inactive. Roy had been supplied with NCI powder, a highly recommended lice exterminator made of Naphthalene, Camphor and Iodoform. After spreading his blanket on the ground, he sprinkled it with the unpleasant smelling powder. Hardly had he straightened himself up than he found that the flies had devoured the lot.[49] There was also an incessant struggle with flies at meal times, especially when he had carefully spread a biscuit with jam, swishing the knife wildly to disperse them, but still they alighted before he could get it into his mouth.[50]

The officers favoured an open-air setting for their meals, not so much for hygienic as for practical reasons, there being insufficient material available for covering the area of the main terrace which had been selected for the purpose. The only concessions to formality were a rough table and plank to sit on. There were plenty of Egyptian cigarettes, but as Roy found them too dry, he was pleased to get the occasional Virginian.[51]

---

47 Winn RC *Men May Rise* p59
48 Winn RC *Men May Rise* p60
49 Winn RC *Men May Rise* p60
50 Winn RC *Men May Rise* p40
51 Winn RC *Men May Rise* p42

Roy usually occupied a rough seat cut out of the dirt. It was apt to become flooded when it rained, despite all efforts at draining the hillside behind. There were compensations for the discomfort though as, even on a wet day, stretching before the occupant was the kind of panorama that had inspired the Greek poets. In the distance was the island of Imbros, which overlooked where Poseidon scaled the heights of Samothrace so that he might watch the changing fortunes in the Trojan War.[52]

There is not much information about Roy's specific medical-related activities on Gallipoli although he must have been busy during his first deployment as wastage due to disease, death and wounds had almost doubled from 5 per cent to 9 per cent of the force in August and September. Later, sickness began to overtake war injuries as the prime cause of medical evacuation.[53]

Flies posed a huge health problem. Although the Anzacs attempted to bury their dead, it was not always possible to retrieve bodies close to the Turkish lines, nor was it feasible to dispose of the thousands of human and animal body parts strewn around several hundreds of hectares of countryside. Faeces, food scraps and dung from mules and horses contributed to producing ideal fly-breeding grounds. The Anzac medical authorities realised the danger and had incinerators built around the area. Proper latrines were dug but were often just open pits with poles across them and exposed to the elements. Hepatitis became an increasing problem.[54]

The novel suggests that Roy's first casualty was an officer who, although he had only been on Gallipoli for 24 hours, had been wounded in the foot while asleep in his dugout.[55] We also know that, along with all medical officers of the Anzac Medical Association, he was invited

---

52 Winn RC *Men May Rise* p61
53 Swifte T *Gallipoli The Incredible Campaign* 1985 p72
54 Swifte T *Gallipoli The Incredible Campaign* 1985 p72
55 Winn RC *Men May Rise* p60

Water fatigue

by Colonel Begg to attend Otago Gully on 5 December for a discussion about the treatment of wounds from the RMOs' perspective. We don't know if he actually attended but, given his Methodist uprightness, assume he did.

Roy took a number of photographs of the field ambulance tents and dugouts at B Section, Walden Grove and Hay Valley. The landscape looks dry and there was a widespread lack of water, which fell hardest on the privates who only got a quart[56] a day. What they could stop themselves from drinking, they used first for cleaning their teeth, then they shaved in the same water and finally had a wash with it.[57] The lack of water contributed to an increase in cases of dysentery, diarrhoea and enteric diseases.

Field Ambulance B Section

---

56   Quart is just under a litre
57   Winn RC *Men May Rise* p40

Above: Dugouts, 4th Field Ambulance *Below*: Field Ambulance Walden Grove

Still, Roy's second taste of war, even on the frontline, was apparently no more unpleasant than the first. Both sides were content to stay in their respective trenches and only snipe when a target appeared.[58]

As the weather became cooler, flocks of birds passed overhead, flying to the warm south. One morning, the Australians awoke to the

---

58 Winn RC *Men May Rise* p63

60 pounder Walden Grove

Anzacs awake to the novel sight of snow

novel sight of a landscape covered with snow. Many of the men began to suffer from the cold and Roy became indignant when he discovered that one of the senior officers was using much-needed blankets to line the walls of his dugout. As Roy was responsible for the health of the men and many of them had only one blanket, he sent in a report but nothing was done about it.[59] After severe storms and a blizzard in November, about 3000 Australians suffering from frostbite and exposure had to be evacuated, but the authorities had other matters on their minds and soon the troops would too: they were to evacuate.

Field Marshal Lord Kitchener, the British Secretary of State for War, made an unannounced visit to Gallipoli on 13 November 1915. Roy did not meet him but took a photograph from some distance away. Not long afterwards, there were some unusual happenings at Anzac Cove. There was an order that for three days no-one was to fire bullets or shells at the Turks; blankets, trench boots and other desirable comforts were to be had for the taking;[60] and there was a continuous procession of empty-handed men heading towards the beach and beasts of burden heading away from it. Something was afoot and there was much speculation. When the men were instructed to dump extra ammunition in the privies and

Lord Kitchener's visit

---

59 Winn RC *Men May Rise* p63
60 These desirable comforts, which had been scarce while the conflict was ongoing, were now no longer being hoarded as evacuation was imminent

told to set up automatically fired rifles in front of the trenches,[61] they knew they were to leave Gallipoli.

Roy was instructed to divide the men into two groups according to physical state. He subsequently learned this was to allow the fittest to be available to fight a rearguard action. He had long known that the proper place for an RMO was at the rear of the battalion. This had been a comforting thought when an attack was under consideration but far from reassuring now that a retreat was planned. His fears were reduced when he heard that his battalion was not to be one of the last to leave.[62]

Roy describes the night of departure as an eerie experience. The half battalion marched single file down the saps[63], the shallow utility trenches, with Roy bringing up the rear. The knowledge that there were only a handful of men holding the trenches gave him a most unpleasant feeling. He wished it were possible to walk backwards. He knew that if the Turks discovered the weakened state of the defences, a holocaust would result, but the remnant of the Anzacs in the trenches fired at a rapid rate in order to make the sound as great as usual. The reason for the three days stoppage of fire was now apparent: it was to prepare the Turks for the day on which the trenches would be held by only a few men.[64]

It was later learned that the Turks thought an attack was being prepared. For days they had observed an increased movement of troops and had not realised the ruse of sending large numbers of troops down to the shore before dawn and then marching them up to the saps in daylight.[65]

When the 14th Battalion finally reached Anzac Cove, Roy observed that every detail was being carried out with great precision, with hardly

---

61 The rifles were to be fired by attaching a string from the trigger to a large tin, which would capsize when filled with water. The water would drip into it from a second tin placed above the first. A clever ruse.
62 Winn RC *Men May Rise* p64
63 A sap is a trench dug at roughly 90 degrees out from existing lines
64 Winn RC *Men May Rise* p64
65 Winn RC *Men May Rise* p65

RMO dugout 14th Battalion

a word spoken. Matting had been laid on the wharf to deaden the sound of horses' hooves and lumbering guns. At 11pm on 18 December 1915 Roy marched behind the others to a shallow-draught launch with a drawbridge stern, which was set against the edge of the wharf. The lighters had been specially designed for service at Gallipoli. Roy was relieved when they passed through the danger zone of stray bullets without anyone being hit.

Eventually the lighter drew alongside a steamer and everyone scrambled aboard. The crew gave a rousing welcome. The skipper offered cigars. The padre contributed a couple of bottles of whisky.[66] The ferry steamed to Mudros Harbour and eventually the men were transferred to a battle cruiser that would carry them back to Egypt. Every soldier was entertained by someone of corresponding rank among the crew, the ship's surgeon providing Roy with a hot shower and then conducting him to a four-course breakfast served on tablecloths. Before Roy enlisted, he was asked to join the navy. For the first time, he wondered whether he had made a mistake in not doing so.[67]

---

66   Winn RC *Men May Rise* p65
67   Winn RC *Men May Rise* p65

A total of 142 000 men were evacuated from Gallipoli in what is considered a stunningly successful operation. The Gallipoli Campaign preceding it had been a heroic but costly failure, with over 26 000 Australian casualties, and 363 officers and 7779 men killed. At the time, Australia's population was less than five million. Nine Australians were awarded the Victoria Cross.

The cruiser docked in Alexandria on 2 January 1916. Roy's brigade then travelled overland to the Suez Canal, where its members were to defend Egypt against the threat of Turkish invasion through Palestine, an even greater possibility now that the Turkish troops who had occupied Gallipoli were free to attack elsewhere.[68] At Ismailia, Roy received his first mail, which took two days to read, and his cabin trunk from army stores, which furnished him with a clean uniform.

At 4am on 27 February 1916 the brigade moved to Tel El Kebir as part of a military reorganisation. A month later, they were at Serapeum after a three-day journey that would never be forgotten by those who took part in it.

It was decided that the troops were not to travel to Serapeum by train but to march, so that they would become inured to desert conditions.[69] They commenced at 10pm on 31 May 1916. The heat of the day was like a furnace, the hottest Roy had ever experienced. The first day's journey was along a dusty road which bordered a

Felucca at Tel El Kebir

---

68   Winn RC *Men May Rise* p71
69   Winn RC *Men May Rise* p73

freshwater canal. Roy spent his time riding up and down the line trying to prevent the men from drinking the water for fear of infestation with dangerous parasites. At night, the battalion bivouacked in the open air as the tents had been sent ahead by train. It was bitterly cold.

The second day was worse. It was hotter than the previous one and the route was through soft sand. Every step was an effort. The surface was no longer level but broken by huge sand dunes, which often ended in steep slopes. As the ambulance wagons had also been sent to Serapeum by train, Roy had to give up his horse to a man who had collapsed.

Roy could not imagine there could be anything more gruelling to endure but, from the middle of the third day, the path narrowed onto a causeway and the men had to march much closer together. There was hardly a breath of air between the ranks. The route ran parallel to the railway line, along which travelled the tents, horse wagons and ambulances. The horses were too valuable to risk but not so the human beasts, who were required to march laden with full equipment. Men fell by the roadside too tired to take another step. Roy was so exhausted he could hardly think. By evening, even the most placid men were swearing at the idiocy of those who had ordered such an unnecessary test without adequate training.

When the 14th Battalion finally crawled into camp, water was not immediately available for the troops. Happily, a friend gave Roy some Egyptian beer – the most satisfying drink he had ever tasted.[70]

The camp at Serapeum was one of many guarding the Suez Canal. As it was only a mile from the Red Sea, the troops swam regularly. Roy excelled at this sport and tried to never miss a bathing parade. As on Gallipoli, no bathing costumes were required though they would have been an advantage when passenger ships passed. The Canal varied in width from 100 to 200 yards and it was the custom to swim across it and back many times. Several weeks after arrival, a sports carnival was

---

70 Winn RC *Men May Rise* p74

held, attended by the Prince of Wales who distributed prizes to the winners. Roy came second in a race.[71]

For the most part though, life went on without incident except when it was broken by the *Kamsur*[72] – the hot wind that roars across the desert, raising stifling clouds of dust so thick that animals, and occasionally men, would perish. When it blew everyone kept to the tents, but even there it was impossible to avoid eating a liberal ration of grit with every mouthful of food.[73]

At Serapeum Roy had time to write letters home. He often wrote to Ellie McMurtrie, revealing something of his character: 'You know Ellie that I love you though I do not talk much about my sentiments probably because I am too inclined to self-consciousness. This being the case you may rely on my deepest sympathy for the trouble that you infer.'[74] Tantalisingly, we do not know what Ellie's troubles were, but Roy was obviously very fond of her and from the time she married his oldest brother Harold, Roy welcomed her as a sister.

Roy writes playfully about the charm and beauty of the bridesmaids at his second brother Gordon's wedding to Ida McMurtrie, Ellie's sister. He laments that 'the proceedings could not have been completely rounded off by the Bad Boy of the Family…', presumably referring to himself.[75] In the same letter, he speculates that his 'Brother Bill[76] is probably still keeping up his reputation as a tease'. He writes more seriously about the death of Frank Pratt, presumably a mutual friend '… it is glorious that such fine fellows are ready to lay down their lives for an idea and principle'.[77]

He also writes about Egypt: 'I must admit that Egypt is a country that has fascinated me with its life so different to that of Australia.

---

71   Winn RC *Men May Rise* p75
72   Roy probably means the Khamsin wind
73   Winn RC *Men May Rise* p83
74   Winn RC *Letter to Ellie McMurtrie* 8 February 1916
75   Winn RC *Letter to Ellie McMurtrie* 12 January 1917
76   Brother Bill is presumably Roy's oldest brother, Harold
77   Winn RC *Letter to Ellie McMurtrie* 8 February 1916

Roy: writing letters home

The cosmopolitan nature of the people with the resultant advantages and faults makes an interesting study.' He notes differences between national groups. 'We see a lot that is French in origin, the naturalness and demonstrative affection which is so different from the Anglo-Saxon reserve, the assurance of the Australian, and even the boyish impertinence of the Egyptian which is amusing to us who are ready to accept everyone as equals until they show themselves not.' He reflects on the Australians' response to Egypt saying it gives Australians a sense of smallness to visit old mosques and Coptic churches, an experience that will not harm them, but when they visit the pyramids and the romantic Sphinx, they cannot help but be impressed, even though they try to cloak their emotions under a joke.[78]

In April 1916 Roy wrote from Serapeum to his brother,[79] who was also serving in the war, saying he didn't have too much to grumble at, as he had had a long interval free from the fear of bullets and pieces of animated metal. He acknowledged that he felt sad that their 'loved ones

---

78   Winn RC *Letter to Ellie McMurtrie* 14 May 1916
79   Presumably Gordon Winn

are anxious about us while we are far from danger and really spending a wonderful holiday'. The letter mentions that he was reading *Hamlet* and other productions of the Bard and that he remained impressed by Shakespeare's influence on the English language. He had been taking photographs and shot one of a polo match using donkeys. He finishes by reminding his brother that, 'fraternal love is no myth, though not much talked about'.[80]

Donkey polo

Camp life in Egypt gave Roy little opportunity for medical work, apart from sick parades and inspections, spiced with an occasional outbreak of disease. In another letter to Ellie McMurtrie, he wrote, 'we live fairly comfortably in a camp… as we are in reserve and in training. We have an officer's mess and are making health arrangements as permanent as possible as this camp will be used by us and our reinforcements from now on'.[81]

There was a meningitis outbreak a few weeks after their arrival

---

80   Winn RC *Letter to Big Brother* 11 April 1916
81   Winn RC *Letter to Ellie McMurtrie* 8 February 1916

at Serapeum and all ranks were made to march through a tent filled with formalin vapour in an effort to limit its spread. The men's tents were overcrowded and it was considered that increasing the accommodation options would prove a more effective measure than the inhalation treatment. Some people at headquarters, it was discovered, were using a cache of extra tents as bedding, but it was only after numerous complaints were made about this that the extra tents were finally distributed. One of the newly arrived tents presented an amazing sight. In the warm sunlight, hundreds of lice crawled out from under the seams and spread all over the side of the tent. There was no doubt the tent had been used for bedding![82]

Even an outbreak of meningitis was not enough to keep Roy fully occupied. A routine vaccination for the whole battalion was welcomed because it broke the routine monotony of camp life. To fill his spare moments when not swimming or watching donkey races, Roy went on expeditions and visited friends in other battalions. He mentions that he made a trip to a hospital organised by the Church Missionary Society (the original English branch), which interested him immensely. 'To see the natives sitting in a special compound undergoing treatment for Anchylostomiasis[83] was a sight worth remembering. These special dispensations, where the patients may stay until they undergo a cure of two to three weeks, are now being organised all over Egypt as a result of Kitchener being impressed with the results at his old Hospital. The patients looked very funny opening their mouths to have the medicine poured in, like a big nest full of young birds.'[84]

---

82 Winn RC *Men May Rise* p88
83 Hookworm infestation was prevalent in Egypt and a cause of profound anaemia.
84 Winn RC *Letter to Ellie McMurtrie* 14 May 1916

Life in Egypt was not all light-hearted and Roy's poem *Egypt* offers another more sombre view.[85]

> A fireplace heap of glaring human faces
> With tinder in the midst of unborn babe
> Nearby an anklet wrought in antique bronze
> Terrestrial flotsam on a sea of sand
>
> A fellahun who mourned his pregnant wife
> Took comfort when he viewed her resting place
> As from the grave a scarab issued forth
> A symbol this of immortality
>
> A tent of soldiers in a long campaign
> Reduced the boredom with a game of chance
> At sight of moving sand each placed a coin
> Where wag'ring unseen scarab would emerge.

The extant letters to Ellie say little about his time on Gallipoli but hint at its effect: 'I am thankful to say that there are no shells falling about and no strays and snipers for the present. It was not very dreadful there but it was bound to have some effect on the nerves, no matter the constitution.'[86] The novel suggests that Roy was starting to be depressed. He had sleepless nights and alarming dreams. His friends did their best to cheer him up.[87]

---

85 Winn RC Poem 'In Egypt' 20 August 1949
86 Winn RC *Letter to Ellie McMurtrie* 8 February 1916
87 Winn RC *Men May Rise* p76

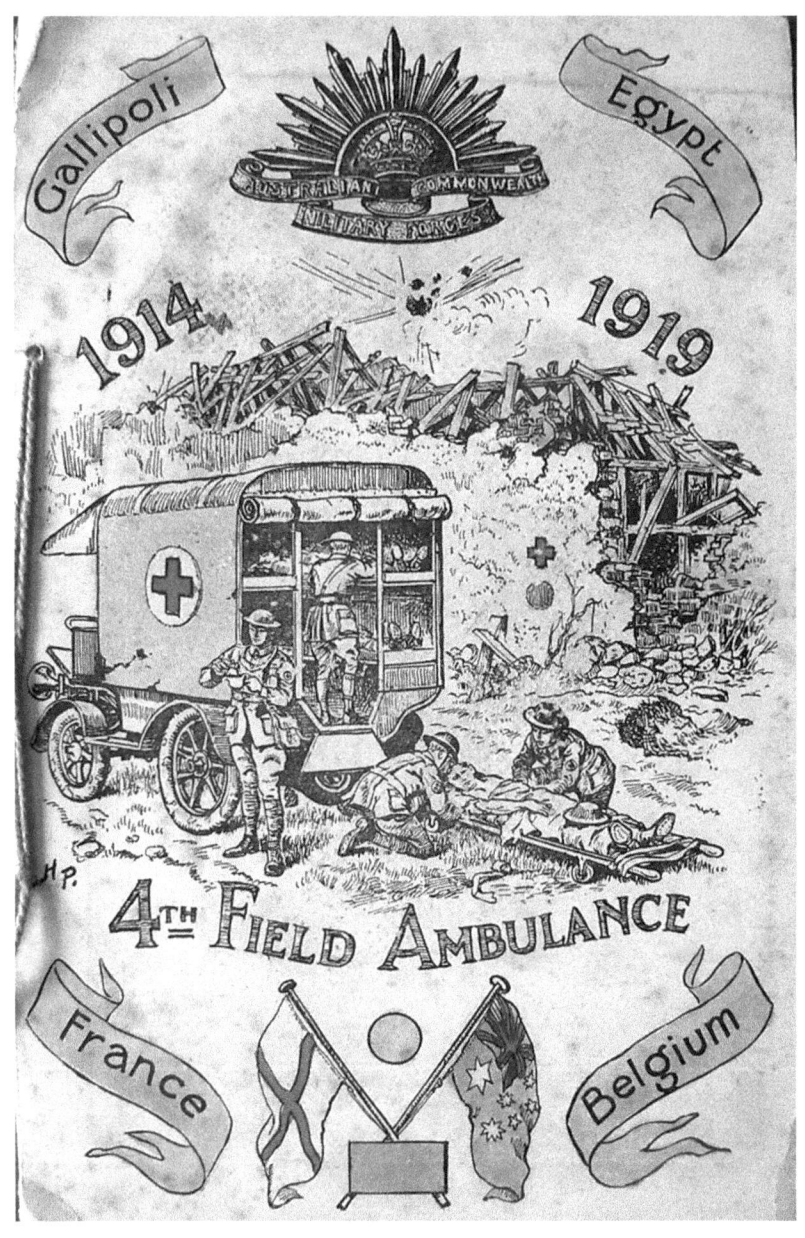

4th Field Ambulance booklet cover

3

The Western Front takes its toll

After six months in Egypt, Roy's battalion sailed for Europe, arriving at Marseilles on 7 June 1916, thankfully without a submarine being sighted. The ship had taken the precaution of following a zigzag route in the day and steaming in total darkness at night – Malta was sighted twice.[88] After a short leave in Marseille, Roy travelled north by train, via Angevin, Lyons and Amiens, towards the Germans and the war zone. His destination was Bailleul in northern France, where he was to stay for a week.

The train trip took three days. Roy's diary mentions an absence of cattle in the south; old men, women and children emptying trucks; washing in the river; and rather poor villages.[89] Stoppages occurred every few miles and, when the train was moving, it moved at walking pace. As a precaution against desertion, it travelled faster through towns and villages than in open country. If it was inadvertently halted in a town, the passengers avidly sought bread, wine, cigarettes, chocolates and biscuits. On the third day, Roy and some friends alighted at Abbeville in the hope of buying newspapers, but were cut off from rejoining their train by another train heading in the opposite direction. The next train for Bailleul did not pass the station until late that night so Roy filled the time by inspecting a hospital train stopped at a side platform. When they finally arrived at their destination, they had to suffer a barrage of

---

88 Winn RC *Men May Rise* p89
89 Winn RC *WWI Diary* 31 July 1915–5 April 1918

Gas-proof dugout at The Bluff, Belgium

chaff over what was claimed to be an attempted desertion.[90]

Roy's 14th Australian Infantry Battalion of the 4th Australian Brigade was fully absorbed into the 4th Division in France. Not many days passed before they were ordered to the frontline. The billeting officer went ahead and he and his men were exposed to their first gas attack. As they had not been issued gas helmets, they were told to soak their socks in water and use them to cover their mouths, an improvisation that proved effective. Next day, everyone was issued with gas helmets and marched through a specially prepared trench full of poison gas. The experience gave everyone confidence in the masks, as there were no ill effects.

A week later, they took over from another battalion. The terrain was flat and trench diggers were vulnerable to enemy fire. As trenches could not be dug, cover was obtained by building a parapet with sandbags. Instead of a dugout, Roy occupied a hut with walls made of sandbags and roofed with iron. Nearby, a similar but larger structure served as

---

90   Winn RC *Men May Rise* p89

his regimental aid post. This surgery was near the main sap, which led to the frontline trenches. Huge rats scurried everywhere at night, even over Roy's face. He soon got accustomed to them but found it harder to overcome his fear of gas.[91]

At this aid post Roy witnessed his first trench raid, designed to capture a few German prisoners in order to collect information. The Australian raiders' faces were blacked and they were armed with fearsome clubs, Mills bombs and revolvers. Unfortunately, the supporting artillery bombardment failed to destroy the German wire entanglements and the enemy's return fire was continuous. The raiders eventually crawled back through no man's land to the Australian trenches, the wounded assisting those who were more seriously wounded. Roy worked for hours before the last casualty passed through his hands and started the long journey to the hospital.[92]

The next night, while Roy was reading in his hut, all hell broke out. It was a box barrage – a continuous wall of bursting shells and aerial torpedoes – and it extended 100 yards along the southern part of the battalion's trenches. There was an incessant roar of explosions for over an hour. It seemed to Roy that no living thing could survive it. Casualties soon arrived at the regimental aid post in such numbers that Roy could not manage them single-handed.[93]

By 24 June 1916, Roy was at Bois Grenier and his work was soon noticed. '… on the night of 4–5 July after an enemy raid on the trench held by his battalion, Roy was in the front line dressing the wounded, and remained there until all had been attended to.'[94]

On 8 July 1916, the 4th Division was ordered south to participate in 'The Push' also known as the Somme Offensive. The Push lasted from

---

91   Winn RC *Men May Rise* p90
92   Winn RC *Men May Rise* p92
93   Winn RC *Men May Rise* p92
94   Likeman R *Gallipoli Doctors* 2010 p145

1 July to 18 November 1916, and involved numerous individual battles on both sides of the upper reaches of the River Somme. Overall, it was the largest battle on the Western Front – over three million men participated and there were a million dead or wounded. Australia alone had 23 000 casualties.

En route south, Roy's battalion came across all that remained of a division that had just returned from one of the Somme Offensive's battles. Roy described their ghastly appearance as pitiful to see, their faces haggard, their eyes staring at unseen horrors, blind to the world of living men.[95] [96] Instead of a thousand men, each battalion had only a few hundred left. Roy knew one of the medical officers trudging along with a handful of men, the remnants of his battalion. He told Roy that he had lost all his stretcher-bearers within the first 24 hours.

Roy's battalion already had 32 stretcher-bearers, which was twice the usual number. Roy got permission to train half as many again and, not content with that, to give an equal number of men a short course in first aid. Before Roy's battalion took its part in The Push, over 60 men were capable of rendering a measure of surgical aid to their fellows.[97]

In mid-1916, the German line extended from Mouquet Farm in the north, ran behind Pozières to the east and then south towards the Bazentin Ridge. Mouquet Farm was a strong point, which so far had resisted capture, being fortified with pillboxes[98] connected to each other by underground passages.[99]

On 6 August Roy's battalion was ordered to take Mouquet Farm. On the night of Roy's arrival, a half company of the battalion was ordered to attack. There was scarcely a survivor, and the subsequent German bombardment produced many casualties in the trenches. It was clear that the British had no idea of the strength of the German

---

95   Winn RC *Men May Rise* p93
96   Bean C *Official History of WWI* Vol. III p598
97   Bean C *Official History of WWI* Vol. III p598
98   Reinforced concrete guard house
99   Winn RC *Men May Rise* p116

defences: it subsequently took an entire brigade to take the Farm[100] after a number of attacks and counter attacks, the Australians having been repulsed at least three times.[101]

Roy used a dugout as his first aid post. It was 10 feet underground and stretcher-bearers could easily descend the steps. Unlike at Pozières later, where he could only use a torch, at Mouquet Farm his entrance shaft faced away from the enemy so he was able to use as much illumination as he wished. He improvised an operating table by setting up supports on which the stretchers could be placed.[102]

After Mouquet Farm, on a perfect summer day, the 14th Battalion made its way to Pozières on the Albert-Bapaume Road. It was to engage the enemy near 'The Windmill' from 7 to 13 August 1916, in what was recorded as a period of intense and violent frontline fighting.[103]

The route passed huge 12-inch guns in great number and enormous shell craters a full hundred yards in width. When the track led through the jauntily named Sausage Gully, howitzers and field guns were seen literally wheel to wheel. As the battalion advanced it was shot at and every gun in Sausage Gully responded. The black smoke of bursting shells and the red dust that arose when they hit the ground, hid the skyline from view. Roy soon learned that the flash of bursting shells over Pozières rarely ceased.[104] Pozières was no longer a quaint village of roofless houses as he had seen further north. Pozières was a heap of red dust.

The 14th Battalion headquarters was in a dugout which had originally been built to house German military staff, a fact which was exemplified by the elaborateness of the fittings and the strength of its timbering. It was fully 20 feet deep. The main entrance had been demolished, which was fortunate as it faced the enemy. Another shaft,

---

100   Winn RC *Men May Rise* p116
101   Company had 100–200 men, battalion 500–800 and brigade 1500–4000
102   Winn RC *Men May Rise* p116
103   Wanliss N *History of the 14th Battalion* p147
104   Winn RC *Men May Rise* p93

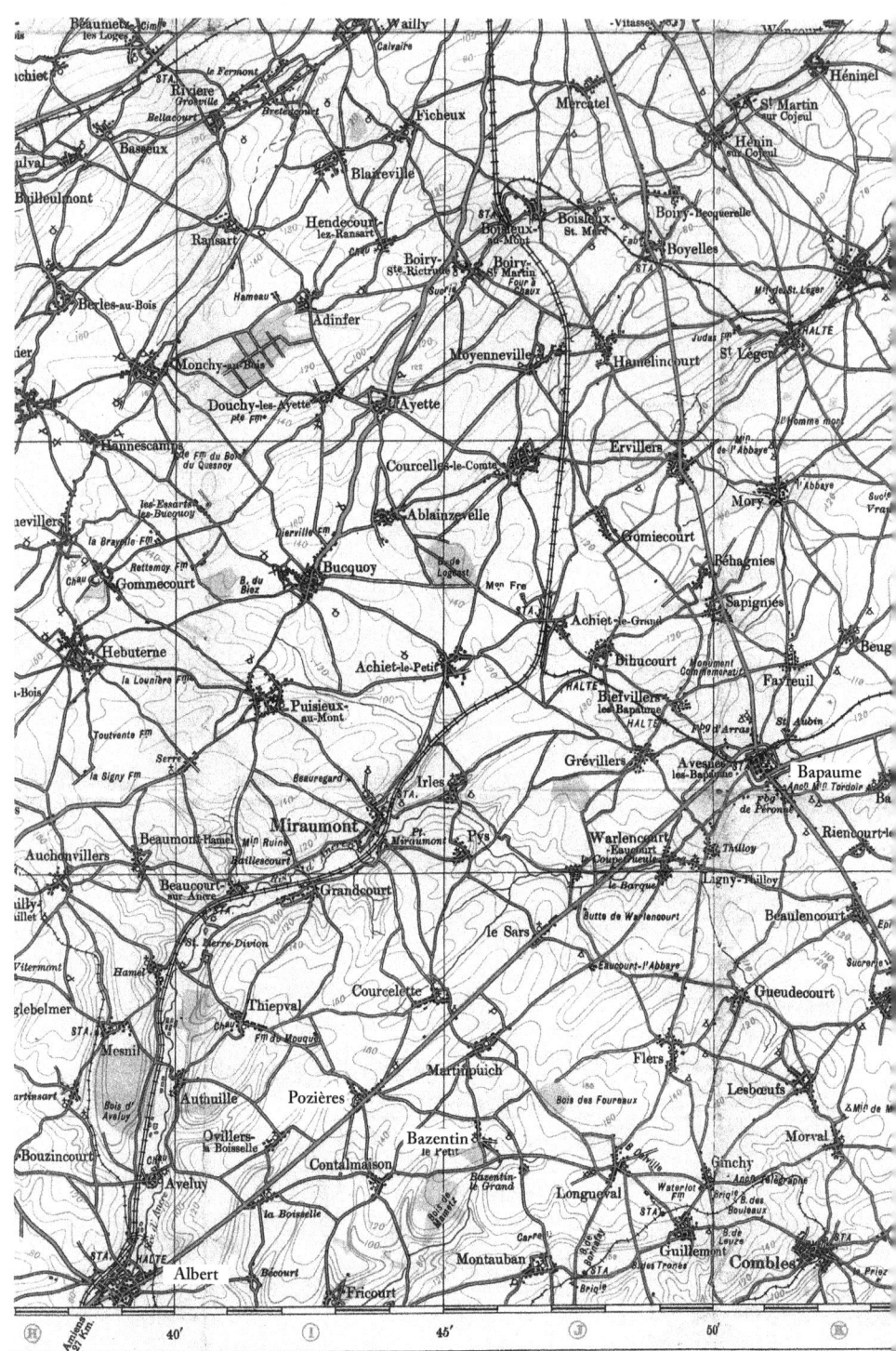

Roy's WWI map of Pozières

built for ventilation, was used as the new entrance, but this shaft did not have steps, so climbing in and out was difficult. Roy was given a bunk in a small alcove near the entrance shaft.

Roy knew that the dugout's precise location would be on German maps and, sure enough, it was always given special attention whenever a bombardment started. Roy was supposed to site his regimental aid post inside this dugout but it was clearly unsuitable as stretcher cases could not be taken below.

Roy looked for a more suitable site. In one sap he explored, he saw a recently killed man. Not wanting him to become another bloated corpse, Roy lifted the body over the side. He must have been silhouetted against the sky, for a barrage commenced immediately. He scrambled down into the sap and crouched low as shell after shell exploded around him. He then ran as fast as he could towards his own dugout half a mile away. The shells followed and his foot was slightly wounded. 'The Huns are searching for me,' he thought. 'They can't kill me' and laughed hysterically.[105]

Roy never did find a suitable site and settled for working in the sap at the entrance of the dugout. He worried less when he was in the sap, despite the shells.[106]

He could not sleep that first night as he couldn't take his mind off the fact that the Huns had the exact range of the dugout and used it whenever they started a bombardment. Some explosions were louder and more terrifying than others, making the dugout and his bunk rock, and dislodging earth, which fell through the crevices between the supporting planks and pattered on the floor. The shells varied in size from 'pip squeaks' to the 'trains' of the large siege guns. The majority were either 'five nines' or 'nine-inch shells.' Each concussion of the larger shells not only threatened to burst his eardrums but also seemed to press down on his skull with unbearable force. Even in the intervals between them, there was little relief. The short silences seemed like

---

105 Winn RC *Men May Rise* p97
106 Winn RC *Men May Rise* p103

eternities. The shelling increased throughout the night for over eight hours until the pounding became incessant. Roy wondered how men in the frontline could survive such a maelstrom without any protection whatsoever.[107]

As dawn broke, the shelling lessened and finally came to an end, to be followed by waves of men in grey uniforms attacking. Hand-to-hand fighting erupted between grey and khaki, until khaki prevailed. The British artillery opened fire and laid a barrage in the distance to prevent a counter attack. While Roy was attending to the wounded (both German and Australian), the Germans opened a barrage on the sap. Many men were again wounded. Among them was a lieutenant who had started out with 52 men but, after the shelling and hand-to-hand fighting, was left with only seven.[108]

In addition to what Roy described in his novel above, he wrote his own version on the clearance of the wounded at Pozières for the official record. 'The aid post was a deep German dugout. Two regimental officers worked in a sap near the entrance. This was moreover choked with wounded, many of whom would be wounded afresh or killed outright while being attended to. The earth for miles behind the line was like a ploughed field and changed like the waters of a rain-swept lake. The dugout rocked with concussion. Many wounded were brought in who had been out days before being rescued. Some of their wounds were crawling with maggots but looked surprisingly clean.'[109]

Both the matter-of-fact style of official military reporting, and the understated descriptions found in Roy's novel, make it hard to fully appreciate the ferocity of the battle and the extreme conditions under which Roy worked. The 6-13 August Battle of Pozières was considered to be the worst bombardment that had ever fallen on Australian troops. The 4th Australian Division ultimately lost 7100 men. On the

---

107 Winn RC *Men May Rise* p94
108 Winn RC *Men May Rise* p96
109 Butler AG *Official History of Australian Army Medical Services 1914–1918* Vol. II p63

second day, Roy's 14th Battalion lost 20 per cent of its personnel.[110] For seven days straight, Roy worked with only one other doctor. The two of them were as close to the frontline as one could get,[111] attending to unheard of numbers of casualties in an exposed sap, which was bombarded ceaselessly. The noise levels and concussion shocks were extreme. They did not manage more than two hours sleep every 24.[112] They were exhausted.

The authorities recognised the heroic effort and Roy was mentioned in despatches. 'This officer worked unceasingly with little rest and in an exposed position continually subject to enemy shell fire, being twice slightly wounded.'[113] But it did not come without a personal cost, as Roy's novel makes clear.

In *Men May Rise* Roy describes the experience of war at Pozières. Day succeeded day, each like the preceding one, the same toll of killed and wounded, the same ear-splitting sounds, the same horrifying sights, the same penetrating smells of death and destruction. Men struggled to the regimental aid post from the frontline on trembling legs, hardly able to support their tired bodies. Roy did not have to evacuate all such cases as some recovered after a few hours rest in the dugout, but the faces of the survivors became increasingly haggard, the dark stubble of uncut beards emphasising the pallor from loss of sleep and ever-present dread.[114]

Like his patients, Roy also suffered from dread and loss of sleep. Like his patients, he was not immune to their consequences. 'At Pozières I had been very close to shell shock and carried on under intense strain even afterwards. Loss of sleep was, in my opinion, one of the worst contributing factors which precipitates a breakdown under shellfire and this should be prevented if it is humanly possible to do so. Short

---

110 Wanliss N *History of the 14th Battalion* p147
111 Travers RC *personal communication* 2019
112 Winn RC *Men May Rise* p102
113 *London Gazette* 2nd Supplement No.29890 2 January 1917 and *Commonwealth Gazette* No.103 29 June 1917
114 Winn RC *Men May Rise* p98

terms of service in the line is the best way to counter it, of course, but this may not be practicable.'[115] Roy in fact did manage to short circuit evacuation due to shell shock by providing temporary rest and recuperation for his patients at Pozières. This treatment was also put into practice on organised medical lines by the RMO of 48th Battalion.[116] [117]

At his aid post, Roy noted that the wounded arrived bleeding, despite the use of tourniquets. 'He found that the tourniquet, by obstructing the venous circulation, in fact promoted bleeding, which he stopped by removing the constriction.'[118] It is not clear whether this was Roy's independent observation or if it was seen as a major advance in battlefield first aid at the time. However, from this time, coordinated efforts were made to appreciate the dangers of tourniquets and their narrow time factor of safety. Eventually the use of tourniquets gave way to plugging: local pressure by bandage and haemostatic forceps left in situ by the RMO.[119]

Roy is also reported to have developed new treatments for the potentially fatal medical condition called 'trench foot', caused when the soldiers' feet had been wet for too long.[120] The result of such exposure was loss of circulation and nerve function, which could lead to infection, tissue death, gangrene and amputation. The British recorded up to 75 000 trench foot-related casualties over the course of the war and it was seen as a significant problem. Standard medical treatment appears to have been bed rest and foot washes with lead and opium. However, Roy's war diary details trench foot prophylaxis and treatment using specific doses of powdered camphor, camphorated oil and sodium borate for both mild and severe cases. It is not clear if he devised this particular treatment independently.

---

115 Butler AG *Official History of Australian Army Medical Services 1914–1918* Vol. III p105
116 Butler AG *Official History of Australian Army Medical Services 1914–1918* Vol. III p105
117 Damousi J *Freud in the Antipodes* 2005 p34 – at war's end 800 000 British soldiers had been diagnosed with shell shock
118 Butler AG *Official History of Australian Army Medical Services 1914–1918* Vol. III p347
119 Butler AG *Official History of Australian Army Medical Services 1914–1918* Vol. III p347
120 Sanders A in C. Chapman (ed) *Inner Worlds: Portraits and Psychology* National Portrait Gallery Canberra 2011 p123

After the decimation of Roy's battalion at Pozières, it was finally relieved by another and was marched to a hill near Albert where they bivouacked under the stars. Because he had broken his spectacles, Roy was given permission to go to the eye department of the military hospital in Amiens. While there, he lunched on fish with mushroom sauce at one of its famous restaurants. He considered it a triumph of culinary art.[121]

It was certainly a change from the food at the Pozières front, though miraculously, hot food had reached the frontline every day during the period of unprecedented shelling, a testament to both organisation and courage. Fatigue parties carried stew and tea in empty petrol cans which unfortunately were not always free of petrol fumes. Occasionally, the stew and tea were in the same tin.[122]

Roy's gentle brand of humour in the face of war is further evident in his war diary where he records his medical maxims:
- » Have patients
- » A fee in the hand is worth two on the books
- » Let your X-rays so shine that you may see their bad works
- » Better a dead patient than a live appendix

Typical of the man, the diary also lists detailed treatments for wounds, ambulance shock, trench foot, use of tourniquets and cleaning the hospital.

Roy rejoined his battalion at Dickebusch, a village its civilians had been forced to evacuate because of the shelling. He was allocated a basement room, which was reasonably dry despite the incompleteness of its roof. His duties required him to visit the frontline where even the 'pip squeaks' would startle him, as he had not yet recovered from the strain of Pozières and Mouquet Farm.[123]

The next sector the 14th Battalion occupied was Hill 60. There, no

---

121 Winn RC *Men May Rise* p115
122 Winn RC *Men May Rise* p97
123 Winn RC *Men May Rise* p134

Dickebusch

man's land was only 20 yards wide at the narrowest part. Rifle grenades were largely used as offensive weapons but, in addition, trench mortars hurled huge bombs. The German 'rum jars' could be sometimes avoided in daylight because they were visible when in flight and British troops retaliated with 'plum puddings'. [124] This sector was also known for its mining operations, each side digging tunnels in the hope of blowing their enemy to destruction from underground. It was also especially dangerous for poison gas, and so respirators were never out of easy reach and the regimental aid post dugout was made gas-proof. Everyone was relieved when the battalion marched out after only a week.[125]

While he was out of the line, Roy vaccinated the occupants of a nearby prisoner-of-war camp. As they stood waiting their turn, many of the once arrogant Germans fainted, which pleased him.[126]

---

124 Winn RC *Men May Rise* p134
125 Winn RC *Men May Rise* p134
126 Winn RC *Men May Rise* p135

After the severe losses of Australian soldiers in the Somme Offensive, particularly those inflicted at Pozières, the Australian government sought to introduce conscription by plebiscite. General Birdwood, the Australian commander, made a personal appeal to the troops to support this initiative and, before returning to the trenches, the Australians voted on the issue. Roy was surprised that the majority were opposed to it but judged that, being volunteers, they did not want conscripts fighting alongside them. This may have been the case, although the more common reason given is that they were reluctant to see additional young men subjected to the horrors of piecemeal and ill-prepared attacks, like the ones they had witnessed on the Somme.

In May 1917 Roy wrote to his parents about Lieutenant Albert Jacka's views about conscription. Roy knew Jacka, who was awarded the Victoria Cross for his actions during the Gallipoli Campaign. It had been rumoured that Jacka supported the anti-conscription party and Roy asked him if it was true. Jacka said 'no' and that when he was in hospital, he had signed a testimonial in favour of conscription.[127]

Albert Jacka VC (right)

---

127 *Sydney Morning Herald* 20 May 1917

Roy's return to the line towards the end of 1916 was memorable. French omnibuses driven by romantic-looking uniformed Zouaves[128] drove his group to their place of bivouac at a place called Sydney Camp. The camp was made up of huts constructed from arches of corrugated iron so strongly constructed as to resist some of the shellfire. The downside was that as winter was approaching, they afforded little protection against the cold. Despite the use of braziers, even the food, including the bread, would be frozen solid during frosty nights and have to be thawed before eating.[129]

Although the cold was unpleasant, the winter weather was welcomed because it often made the usual muddy quagmire into a solid foothold. Before the frosts arrived, Sydney Camp was so muddy that it became known as Sydney Harbour.[130] In some of the forward areas, the mud was so sticky it was hardly possible to move. Rubber waders were issued to the troops to protect their feet from frostbite, but they became stuck in the mud and had to be discarded in favour of stockinged feet. Roy often occupied his spare time drying waders and socks so that at least some of the men might avoid being frostbitten.[131]

The next camp the 14th Battalion occupied was at Bazentin, followed by one in the vicinity of Flers. Here, they prepared to attack Stony Trench. Days of rain left the mud as tenacious as ever. After a preliminary bombardment, the Australians scrambled out of their trenches and either slithered around the edges of shell holes or sank to their waists in mud as they forced their way forward in the teeth of intense machine gun and shell fire. Although they took Stony Trench, that was only the beginning. All night long the fighting went on, counter attack following counter attack, until the Australians finally prevailed and Roy got a break.

---

128   Zouaves were French Algerian corps who retained their exotic uniforms
129   Winn RC *Men May Rise* p135
130   Winn RC *Men May Rise* p135
131   Winn RC *Men May Rise* p136

From 21 October for ten days Roy had his first leave in London. His diary indicates he filled every minute. He visited the main tourist sites such as Hyde Park, St Paul's, the Tower of London, and the Houses of Parliament but also Cheapside and Ludgate. When he approached Westminster Abbey, he could hear the organ and was drawn inside. He was impressed by the gloomy beauty but disgusted by the overcrowded memorials. He came to the conclusion that the size of memorials is in inverse proportion to the fame of the men they commemorate.[132]

Visiting the famous tourist sites is to be expected but what is more interesting to note is that Roy went to the Wesley Chapel in City Road on the first day, the Wesleyan Mission Hall the following day, John Wesley's house the fourth day, and a church service on Sunday morning. He also visited No 3 and No 4 General Hospitals, spent most evenings at the Savoy and Lyric Theatres or dancing, and made a flying visit to Edinburgh and Glasgow.[133] The Wesley focus suggests he still saw himself as part of the Methodist fold but, given all the dancing, perhaps his adherence to its strict tenets was starting to waver.

After leave in England, in December 1916, Roy was formally transferred to 4th Field Ambulance[134] and was allotted a magnificent thoroughbred horse whose stamina matched its appearance. Roy had been 13 months as RMO with the 14th Battalion and hoped he might now obtain more professional experience in his new appointment. On his first route march at the head of his section, the stretcher-bearers decided to try him on and marched in a slovenly manner. Roy warned them: if they did not improve, he would lengthen the route. There was no change and he was compelled to carry out his threat. There was no insubordination again.[135]

---

132 Winn RC *Men May Rise* p119
133 Winn RC *WWI Diary* 31 July 1915 to 5 April 1918
134 As well as RMO of 14th Battalion, Roy appears to have been temporarily attached to the 4th Field Ambulance from December 1915
135 Winn RC *Men May Rise* p137

A January 1917 letter to Ellie McMurtrie included a description of his work with the field ambulance and a quip about him progressing to be surgeon-general. It jokingly reads 'I have made one step in that direction by joining the field ambulance and in taking temporary charge of a Section. When OC of the Section, the kingpin in medical circles of the Division, complimented us on our showing: a larger size in hats please.'[136] Roy wrote the January letter from the mess room of a sister ambulance unit (12th) to which he was attached as bearer captain, one of three in the 4th Field Ambulance. His job was to take charge of about 30 men and do forward medical and surgical work between the RMO and the main dressing station. He writes that 'it is not quite as dangerous as the old job and it is easily more comfortable. Another great advantage of the Amb work is the use of Ambulance cars and, as inferred before, the insight into another branch of the service gives a better chance of promotion...' Clearly, Roy had some ambition but as the earlier 'larger hat' letter implies, he mocked himself for having it.

Despite Roy's jollity, it was not all plain sailing. As Roy's division marched towards Bapaume, which had been abandoned by the Germans when they retreated to the Hindenburg Line, a German aeroplane dropped three bombs on the camp and one of them fell on the horse lines. Mangled horseflesh was everywhere but to Roy's great relief, his horse was unhurt.

On 11 April 1917, Roy's brigade was almost annihilated in an attack on the Hindenburg Line at Bullecourt. The German defenses were deep and strong, with cleverly placed machine guns covering the lines of approach.

The 4th Division, as part of the British 5th Army, was given the task of breaching the line – uniquely, using tanks. Instead of the usual artillery preparation, the Australians were ordered to advance across

---

· 136 Winn RC *Letter to Ellie McMurtrie* 12 January 1917

open ground, into heavy fire, protected by 12 tanks that were to destroy the barbed wire as they went. For some of the troops, it was their first encounter with these novel, barely tested weapons. Roy thought the attack might have proved successful if the tanks had cooperated satisfactorily, but by 4.30am on the morning of the attack, only three tanks had arrived in position. The tanks were so slow that infantrymen overtook them and advanced into murderous fire. They struggled to get through the barbed wire and along the passages covered by machine guns. As the late tanks arrived, they attracted heavy enemy fire. None reached the wire before the infantry.

Despite this, the Australians captured what was thought to be an impregnable position but they were unable to hold it. Machine gun fire from the flank prevented any more supplies of ammunition crossing no man's land and when the men's own ammunition was exhausted, they had to retire through crossfire. The losses were appalling. A thousand returned out of 4000 and only nine officers survived out of 80.[137] Official documents say the 4th Brigade suffered the most, with 2339 casualties out of 3000.[138] The attack had been a costly disaster.

Roy was stationed in a sunken road, which had once been the village of Noreuil. He ran an advanced dressing station from which he controlled the stretcher-bearers. The road was under shellfire but he walked around as if it were Piccadilly. By now, he had acquired a fatalistic attitude which prevented him from seeking shelter, even when it was unnecessary to expose himself.[139]

Despite the April repulse, the Australians were again ordered to attack the enemy line at Bullecourt 22 days later, on 3 May 1917. This time, artillery support was provided and there were no tanks. The fighting was hard and the losses heavy, but the enemy line was penetrated. Finally, the Germans gave up this short section of the Hindenburg Line and fighting ceased after 17 days, on 20 May 1917. But the

---

137 Winn RC *Men May Rise* p138
138 Beveridge G *Western Front Battlefield Tour Guide* Australian War Memorial undated
139 Winn RC *Men May Rise* p138

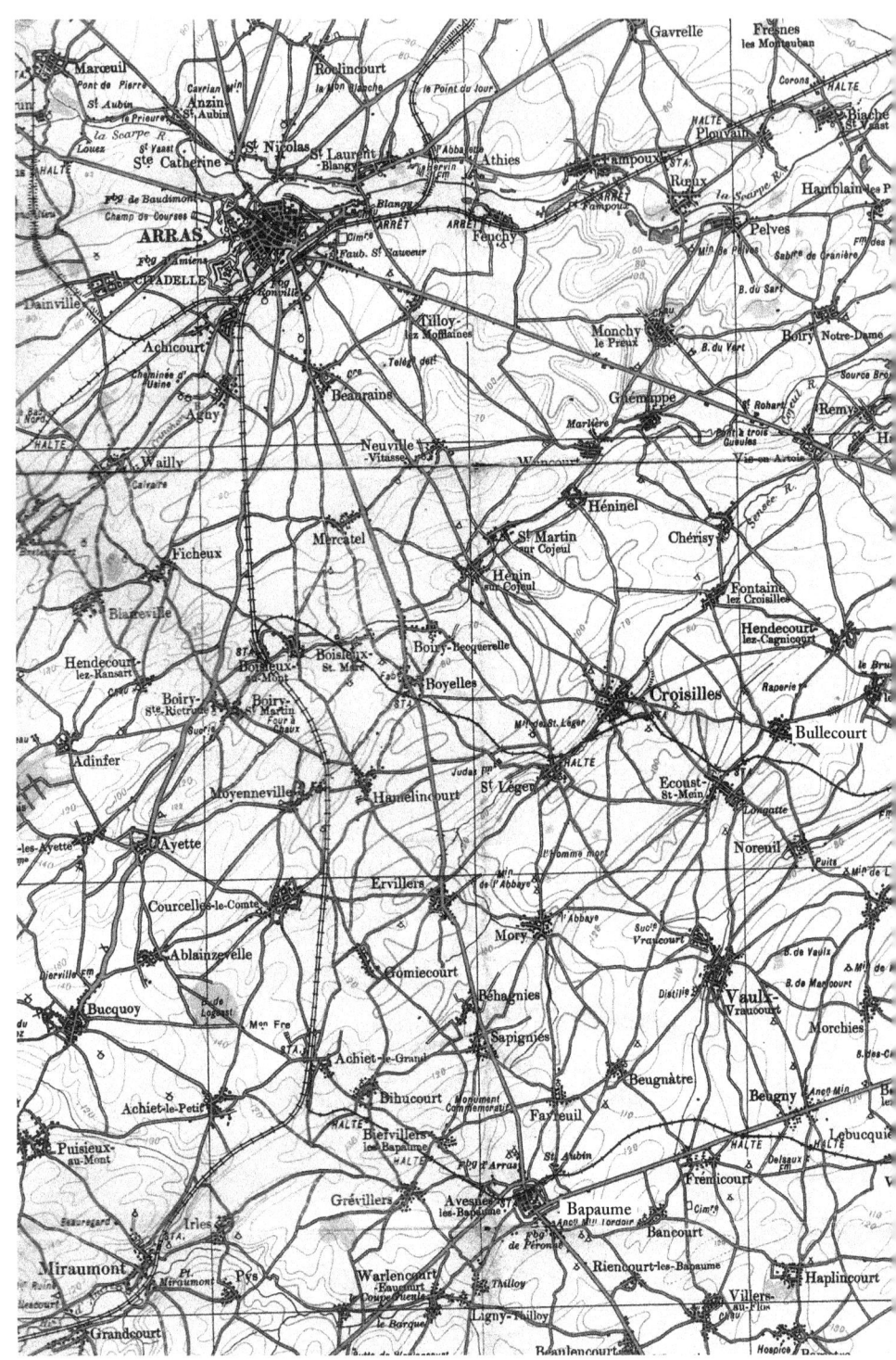

Roy's WWI map of Bullecourt

Australian losses were so severe, they could not exploit their success, and so, no great strategic advantage came of it. The Second Battle of Bullecourt cost the Australians a further 7000 casualties. Charles Bean, the official historian commented that Bullecourt shook the confidence of Australian soldiers in the capacity of the British command. He also wrote that, the Second Bullecourt [battle] was, in some ways, the stoutest achievement of the Australian soldier in France.[140]

The tired and depleted 4th Division moved north to a rest area for the longest break from fighting they had enjoyed since arriving in France. Roy's brigade returned to Ribemont and Roy was touched by the sympathy shown by the French inhabitants over the severe losses. While there, he was asked to attend a French woman in childbirth. Life goes on.[141]

In May 1917 Roy had his second leave in England. His small war diary entries show that he was very busy sightseeing, eating regularly at the Café Royal, attending plays and musicals, buying presents for his family and meeting various friends and young women including, on the 18th, Miss Betty Brown[142] who joined him at the New Theatre to see *The Old Lady Shows her Medals.*

After a month's rest, during which reinforcements swelled the depleted battalions, the 4th Division was sent north to the vicinity of Ypres where there were intensive preparations for the Battle of Messines in June 1917.

Messines stands on a commanding ridge just over six miles (10 kilometres) from Ypres. In November 1914, it had been captured by the Germans and given deep and strong defenses. It was finally re-captured on 7 June 1917, in a well-planned attack that included both the 3rd and 4th Australian Divisions. The 3rd Division was commanded by Major-General John Monash and it was going into a major battle under

---

140 Bean Charles *Official History of WWI* 1921–43, Vol IV chapters 8–13
141 Winn RC *Men May Rise* p138
142 Betty was the nickname Roy gave to Bertha Browne

an Australian general for the first time. Nineteen huge mines were exploded under the German positions to support the heavy shelling that preceded the attack – some of those mines had been in preparation for a year. The Germans were over-run. It was an important victory for the Allies, and a prelude to the 3rd Battle of Ypres.

The Battle of Messines is described extensively in Roy's novel. All the troops were given an opportunity to learn the configuration of the landscape over which they would attack. This was done using a large relief map on which was a pile of earth, fully ten yards long, representing the Messines Ridge. Rumours were current that an enormous mine was to be exploded, the biggest that had ever been prepared. Roy's brigade was to form part of the second wave of the attack and the 4th Field Ambulance was to be held in reserve until the second day.[143]

Roy was asleep in a canvas hut three miles behind the frontline when zero hour arrived. A terrific explosion awoke him – he thought it was the firing of an enormous gun near Neuve Eglise. Other guns joined in and the roar became practically continuous. His camp stretcher rocked, his lamp fell off its box, and the hut creaked and shook like an earthquake. Later, he learned that the initial explosion was actually caused by the firing of a huge mine but, as he was so far away, it took some time for the shock waves to reach him. He tried to imagine what a terrifying thing it must have been for those in the trenches.

Next morning, the 4th Field Ambulance entered the line.[144] Supplied with a guide from the ambulance men being relieved, Roy familiarised himself with the terrain. He made his way across what 24 hours previously had been no man's land. Then he went up the long slope to the headquarters of the battalion, housed in a pillbox captured from the Germans, which had weathered the bombardment. A smaller pillbox nearby was occupied by a group of stretcher-bearers. Roy was to lead them to a glut of wounded at the front. He went to make inquiries about the location of the regimental aid post to which he was headed.

---

143   Winn RC *Men May Rise* p162
144   Winn RC *Men May Rise* p162

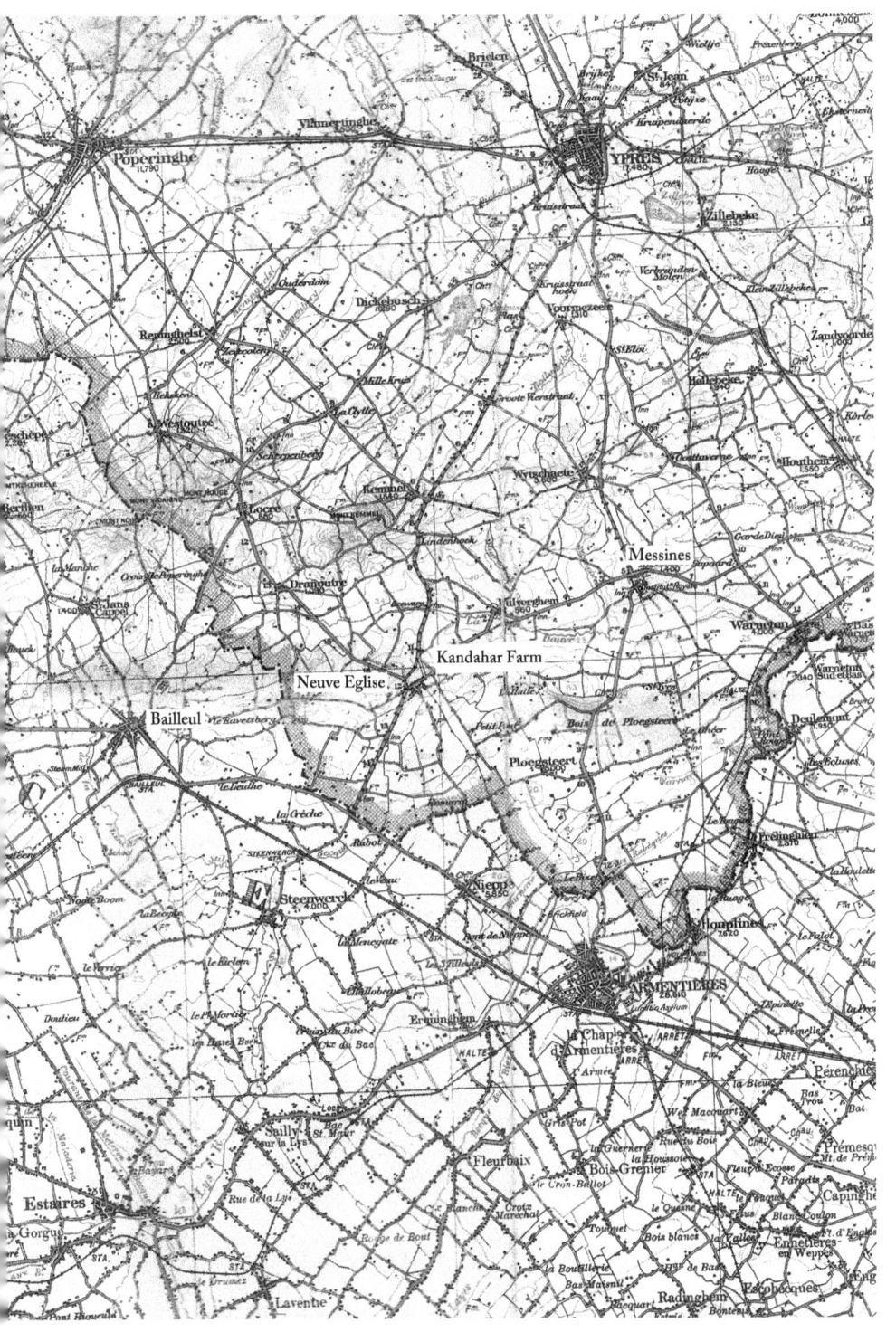

Roy's WWI map of Messines

He discovered it was over the summit and half a mile further on, but when he returned to the small pillbox to lead the bearers forward, a shell had wiped them all out.[145]

Roy then collected 24 new stretcher-bearers from the advanced dressing station and led them to the front line, copping a barrage on the way. A fragment of shell case struck his eyebrow and blood oozed down his face. As Roy led his long line of bearers over the ridge, a machine gun stuttered. *Zip, zip, zip* sounded the bullets as the men all ran for cover. A short distance down the forward slope, Roy found a large shell hole, covered only with two planks of wood, and numerous smaller ones. This was the makeshift aid post of Captain Parker.

A large number of the wounded waited for evacuation, so they loaded them on stretchers and headed back, two wounded to each stretcher. Roy was relieved they made it without a shot being fired at them and was congratulating himself on getting safely through, when

Belgium in ruins

---

145 Winn RC *Men May Rise* p162

a shrapnel shell burst directly overhead. He fell to the ground. There was something wrong with his foot.[146]

The account of his wounding in the novel matches perfectly the official report cited in Likeman's book, which reads, 'Roy was in charge of stretcher bearers evacuating wounded from the right half of the Divisional front under very heavy enemy fire. On one occasion he took a squad over the open through an intense barrage, to a regimental aid post in front of Messines where there was a temporary glut of wounded: he himself was wounded but continued to carry on until again wounded nearly 24 hours later.'[147]

The novel and the official report are also aligned with Roy's own personal account of his wounding at Messines. 'I was ordered by my section commander to take the bearers to pick up eleven wounded which had accumulated at Captain Parker's regimental aid post 45th Battalion. Near the headquarters pillbox we struck a heavy barrage – a shell splinter cut my eyebrow. As we reached the top of the ridge near the regimental aid post a machine-gun opened fire on us, as we came against the skyline… The regimental aid post was in a large shell crater with two heavy beams across as the only cover. Four stretchers were loaded and we set off back. About twenty yards beyond the ridge I was struck on the right foot by a large piece of shell. Parker took my boot off and the front part of my foot fell back on my ankle.'[148] This occurred on 9 June 1917.

The novel describes how the man who came to Roy's aid had risked his own life by running from his shell hole to attend Roy. He took off the boot, noticed the pallor of his friend's skin and judged that the wound was serious. He was not mistaken. As soon as the boot was removed, the fore part of the foot fell back on Roy's ankle. The whole instep had disappeared. The man applied a shell dressing and ordered the bearers to put Roy on a stretcher and hurry to the rear. There was

---

146 Winn RC *Men May Rise* p163
147 Likeman R *Gallipoli Doctors* 2010 p145
148 Butler AG *Official History of the Australian Army Medical Services 1914–1918* p174

little bleeding, but as soon as the shock wore off, there was a chance of a severe haemorrhage. Roy willed himself not to faint, as he was the only one with a thorough knowledge of the terrain. He gritted his teeth.[149]

Around the time of Roy's wounding 'began a tragic succession of deaths and woundings among the bearer captains'.[150]

Roy had been angry when first wounded but soon had a faint feeling of satisfaction. He managed to ignore the fact that he might die of haemorrhage or infection, and to believe instead that the danger of annihilation had passed. After the Battle of Pozières, he had actually hoped that he might be wounded in such a way as to keep him permanently out of the line and even discussed with himself the relative merits of an amputated arm or leg, deciding on the latter because it would interfere less with his professional activities.[151]

Roy was taken to Kandahar Farm Advanced Dressing Station, where his leg was cleaned up and redressed. Kandahar Farm has changed little since 1917. The bomb craters have been ploughed over and the damage repaired but when we visited, the same family was living in the same house and ran the same farm business. They still give thanks to the Australians. Next to the farm is a small war graves cemetery full of young men who never made it out of the dressing station.

Roy was sent in a Ford ambulance to the main dressing station at Neuve Eglise. The numbness was passing off and every bump in the road produced more pain, every bump worse than the last. By the end of the journey, the pain was almost unbearable. At Neuve Eglise he was assessed as fit to travel, so was put in a Rover Sunbeam ambulance and driven quickly to one of the CCSs or Casualty Clearing Stations around Bailleul. Many serious cases reached the stations within three hours of being wounded.[152] It is not clear whether he was sent to one of the two Australian or three British CCSs in the area, all of them

---

149 Winn RC *Men May Rise* p164
150 Butler AG *Official History of the Australian Army Medical Services 1914–1918* p174
151 Winn RC *Men May Rise* p165
152 Bean C *Official History of WWI* Vol. III p681

Kandahar Farm Advanced Dressing Station

working to full capacity. In a 48-hour period the No. 2 Australian CCS admitted and cleared over 2500 patients.[153]

Once at Bailleul, Roy finally lapsed into unconsciousness while being wheeled into the operating theatre.[154] He was given a Syme amputation – where his foot was removed but his heel pad was saved. After many hours he was put in an ambulance for the short trip to Bailleul Railway Station, where he was carried to a train and his stretcher affixed to a rack in a modified Pullman carriage. He was reminded of the hospital train he had examined less than a year earlier. 'I'm safe now he thought, unless the train is bombed by an aeroplane.'[155]

This was not a fanciful thought. During the Messines Offensive, enemy airmen bombed the No. 1 Australian CCS, wounding some Australian nurses, while at a British CCS there were almost 100 casualties.[156]

The train took him to the English Hospital at Wimereux near

---

153 Bean C *Official History of WWI* Vol. III p681
154 Winn RC *Men May Rise* p165
155 Winn RC *Men May Rise* p165
156 Bean C *Official History of WWI* Vol. III p681

Boulogne, where it was decided that he needed another operation as the wound had become septic (with the bacterial infection, gas gangrene) and he was re-amputated.[157] On 13 June, Roy was evacuated to London on an ex-Channel steamer converted into a hospital ship, stowed in its saloon. He imagined it would be his plight to be torpedoed – again, not a fanciful thought.

Communication back to Australia was quick: by 20 June his father William already knew about the amputation. William wrote to the AIF requesting that any communication with Roy be sent to Winn's Ltd rather than his home address, as Roy's mother had not yet been told of his amputation. William wanted to save her any undue distress until the full facts of Roy's medical condition were known.[158]

On arrival at Dover, Roy was put on a hospital train, and spent some time at the 3rd London General Hospital, where he made a good recovery.[159] He was then taken to Exeter Hospital. Within a fortnight, he was in a party visiting Torquay but the vibration of the car induced

Postcard from Roy with X marking the place of amputation

---

157 Winn RC *Men May Rise* p166
158 Winn William *Letter to AIF* 20 June 1917
159 *Sydney Morning Herald* 2 August 1917

such intolerable itching of his wound that he could hardly restrain himself from tearing off the dressings. His own notes and the occasional photograph record that he spent time socialising at Exeter on 28 June, Surrey on 17 September, and Abingdon from 6 to 15 October.

In November 1917, he was transferred, most likely to Copsley, the 2nd Australian Auxiliary Hospital in Southall, Middlesex, which specialised in caring for amputees and fitting artificial limbs.

By the end of August 1917, Copsley had carried out 611 amputations and supplied 344 prosthetic limbs. The kitchen was managed by the Women's Legion. The canteen was run by volunteers, most of whom were Australian women. Workshops were set up by the Red Cross to help rehabilitate the amputees but there were too few of them and only 10 per cent of amputees could be accommodated. Roy's wound does not appear to have healed, and he was becoming more and more depressed.[160]

Roy was congratulated by Major General Sir H V Cox, the commander

Copsley Hospital

---

160 Winn RC *Men May Rise* p174

of the 4th Australian Division, for 'his good work and devotion to duty in France in July and August 1916', and again 'for his devotion to duty during November and December 1916'. He was also mentioned in Field Marshal Douglas Haig's Despatches in January 1917 for distinguished and gallant services and devotion to duty.[161] Roy was congratulated by Major General E G Sinclair MacLagan, commander of the 4th Australian Division, for his bravery and devotion to duty at Messines in June 1917. He was promoted to major in August 1917.

While still in hospital in Southall, Roy received notification that he had been awarded the Military Cross. This MC was 'for conspicuous gallantry and devotion to duty when in charge of stretcher-bearers. He constantly patrolled the bearer line under heavy shell fire, maintaining communication between aid posts and dressing stations, and on one occasion he took a squad across the open through an intense barrage to an aid post in order to relieve the temporary glut of wounded. He was twice wounded, the second time severely and his gallant conduct was the means of saving many lives'.[162]

He was one of four men from the 4th Field Ambulance to receive an Australian MC during that war. He felt proud but quickly came to the view that, as a non-combatant, he had done little to deserve it when compared to real soldiers, most of whom faced greater risks every time they went to the line.[163]

The Lord Chamberlain sent him a telegram inviting him to Buckingham Palace at 10am on 16 March 1918. It was there, in service dress, that he was awarded the Military Cross by King George V who, over the course of the war, personally conferred over 50 000 medals and decorations.[164]

Roy's novel describes being marshalled into a line with hundreds

---

161 *London Gazette* 2nd Supplement No.29890 2 January 1917
162 AIF Base Records Office *Letter to Roy Winn* 14 January 1918
163 Winn RC *Men May Rise* p168
164 Carter M *The Three Emperors* 2009 p445

of others and slowly getting closer to the king. When he approached, the king shook hands and questioned him about his leg. A court official then pinned the medal onto his tunic and Roy backed away on his crutches, having been coached not to turn his back on royalty.

At Copsley, a 'peg leg' had been made for him. He called it 'Peggy' and initially was proud to walk without crutches, but the next day the stump was so painful and swollen he could not wear it. He became extremely dejected. The cause was investigated and it was decided that he needed another operation. Although he was admitted to hospital for two weeks, it was finally decided not to operate. He became even more depressed and decided to seek out a physician who practised hypnosis, which necessitated a weekly trip to London.[165] Roy was already exploring the newer methods of medical treatment.

One of Roy's doctors suggested that his first peg leg must have been a bad fit and that he should be fitted with a new artificial leg. He called it 'Peggy the Second'. When it was completed, he was unable to wear it for more than an hour at a time, and during the night he suffered severe pain. Whenever he attempted its use, failure was the inevitable result and his depression increased with every failure. His dejected appearance resulted in his name being put down for examination by a medical board at headquarters.[166] He received orders to return to Australia and was repatriated in April 1918. He did not travel alone.

As mentioned, Roy met Bertha Elisabeth Browne, known as Betty, on leave in England, probably in May 1917. There are scant details of their time together – apart from a play on 18 May, there were dinners and opera. He bought her a handkerchief and dahlias and she sent him a signed studio photograph of herself in October 1917. Family lore has it that Bertha volunteered at the amputation hospital, but Roy met her the month before his own amputation and, although it would have been a coincidence if she had already volunteered at the place

---

165   Winn RC *Men May Rise* p174
166   Winn RC *Men May Rise* p182

where he ended up, it cannot be ruled out. She does appear in a photograph at Copsley, alongside Roy who is using crutches but they were already friends by then.

According to the UK births' register, Bertha was born in Loddon, Norfolk on 31 January 1884. Her father was Phillip Browne, a carriage builder and garage owner, and her mother, Clara Crickmore. Bertha was the tenth of 11 children. When Roy met her, she was 5 feet 4 inches tall with large brown eyes, brown hair and an attractive face. She

Bertha Browne October 1917

worked as a supervisor in a munitions factory during the war, and when she left to marry Roy, was presented with two 'illuminated addresses'.

After a brief courtship, during which Roy must have been somewhat preoccupied with the ongoing problems associated with his two amputation operations, he and Bertha were married in London on 23 January 1918. He was 28 and she was a few days shy of 34,[167] or possibly 31 if the marriage certificate is accurate.[168]

Bertha's age at marriage is noteworthy, as unmarried women of her generation were considered 'old maids' in their mid-twenties. Notwithstanding the uncertainty about her real age, she was older than convention allowed. Four years of war carnage had decimated the ranks of marriageable men and marriage conventions were beginning to change. She was one of the ones to avoid the long-term spinsterhood

---

167 UK births' register and Browne family tree show her birth as 31 January 1884
168 Marriage certificate 1918

Copsley: Bertha centre, Roy on her left

so common for her generation. The age gap between Roy and Bertha was significant too, as men commonly married women younger than themselves. Perhaps she didn't like the idea of being considerably older than her new husband so she simply offered a more palatable later birth date on her marriage certificate or, less likely but more charitably, perhaps a transcription error occurred in her birth records.

Roy's novel interweaves Tas's war experience with his romance and marriage to the character called Joy and it devotes chapters to Tas's jealousy and sense of betrayal that Joy had failed to tell him that she had been married before. I was interested in this twist and wondered what prompted its inclusion in the novel. Had Roy been disappointed by one or a number of women before he met Bertha? Had Bertha been married or had an important relationship before she met Roy? I did speculate about all this but could find no record of Bertha having any previous marriage or de facto relationship.

THE CONTINUAL INNER SEARCH

Undated sketch by Roy

4

The Catalyst for the Inner Search

When decommissioned, Roy brought his new wife back to Australia with him via the United States and Canada. He chose not to take a government-funded berth for the homeward leg and instead paid for a passenger liner so he and Bertha could have an extended honeymoon.

On arrival in Sydney, Roy felt pride in its beauty. He was determined not to make his first appearance on crutches, so walked ashore wearing his artificial leg, well aware he would have to discard it after a few hours of pain. Bertha passed examination with flying colours and everyone congratulated him on his choice.[169]

The day after their arrival in Sydney he reported to the barracks and learnt that his commission had ended the day he had set foot on Australian soil. He felt he was no longer wanted but soon realised the ridiculousness of such a thought and congratulated himself on his freedom.[170]

No longer able to wear his uniform, he looked through his old wardrobe but could find none of his old suits; they had been given away and he had to borrow one. He and Bertha then had a few days holiday south of the city in Port Hacking, in a friend's cabin, which was surrounded by water at high tide. Schools of fish would swim by,

---

169 Winn RC *Men May Rise* p188
170 Winn RC *Men May Rise* p189

tempting him to drop his fishing line. This was the start of a life-long engagement with fish and the sea.[171]

On their return from Port Hacking, his father prevailed on him to consult one of the leading surgeons in Sydney. The X-ray of his stump showed that the amputation had not been done properly and the surgeon confirmed that Roy required yet another operation.[172] It was his third.

When he finally awoke from the anaesthetic he had a tremendous pain in his thigh. His father told him that the surgeon had operated on his stump through his thigh but had advised William against telling his son that this was what he had planned to do. Even for the time, it would have been unusual for a surgeon not to discuss the operation with Roy, a fellow doctor. It suggests that Roy's mental state was so fragile that his father had to intervene. The wound again did not heal and it was many months before Roy recovered from the operation. As the weeks passed, his depression increased.[173]

Bertha urged Roy to rent a place instead of continuing to live with his parents at Rockley and he unenthusiastically agreed. She found a cottage with a garden in a beachside suburb and encouraged Roy to garden to keep his mind off himself.[174] It did not seem to help.

One night, William rang excitedly to say that an armistice had been signed at 11am. Although it was night time in Sydney, Roy and Bertha immediately drove to town, blowing the car horn at intervals in chorus with every other car on the road. Crowds, yelling themselves hoarse, paraded the streets, beating tins and clanging bells. The shrill whistles of the harbour ferries added to the pandemonium. '*Cock a doodle do*' tooted the ferries. '*Cock a doodle do*', replied the sirens of the great

---

171   Winn RC *Men May Rise* p189
172   Winn RC *Men May Rise* p190
173   Winn RC *Men May Rise* p190
174   Winn RC *Men May Rise* p191

liners, each blast reverberating like thunder. Roy and Bertha drove to Milsons Point to congratulate his parents. They stayed the night but got little sleep because of the continuing noise.[175]

Soon after Armistice Day, Roy was issued with a new artificial leg. He called it 'Peggy the Third' and joked that he had a harem of Peggys.[176] Unfortunately, it was no better than the first Peggy and the novel suggests that Roy's depression and jealousy over Bertha were taking a toll. Bertha had to travel to Brisbane to attend a sick aunt, which exacerbated Roy's jealousy. She tried to help the situation by avoiding other men and looking for activities to keep Roy busy. She asked him to teach her how to swim. They frequented nearby baths and she progressed quickly. Soon he was teaching her how to ride waves in the surf. Bertha could not always accompany Roy to the beach and he soon made friends with other habitués.[177]

By April 1919, the cold winds meant an end to swimming but a friend persuaded Roy to join him boating. This was followed by many picnics on Shark Island or other beauty spots on Sydney Harbour. Usually they would hire rowing boats but occasionally a launch for longer distances.[178] One day Bertha could not go with Roy and suggested he take one of his friends. Roy declared that the friend would not want to give up limited free time to spend with a cripple.[179]

On another occasion, Roy and Bertha accompanied a fisherman who wished to catch a shark to sell as an exhibit in the aquarium. This experience was so interesting that Roy took other opportunities for shark fishing but it was not until he had been half a dozen times that a second shark was caught.[180]

---

175   Winn RC *Men May Rise* p191
176   Winn RC *Men May Rise* p206
177   Winn RC *Men May Rise* p193
178   Winn RC *Men May Rise* p193
179   Winn RC *Men May Rise* p193
180   Winn RC *Men May Rise* p196

Despite the interest Roy took in fishing, his mental state did not improve and he suffered from insomnia and was a tangle of nerves.[181] When Bertha suggested he should start work, he asserted that he did not possess sufficient confidence to accept the responsibility of a hospital appointment. She then suggested he consult a psychiatrist, who advised him to go away on a fishing holiday.[182] This must have been a very difficult period for Bertha.

By mid-1919 Spanish Influenza had become a full scale epidemic in Australia and many of Roy's medical friends were risking their lives treating cases. Although he did not think he could stick a job and was full of fear that he would fail, Roy applied for a position at Sydney Hospital and was immediately attending influenza patients.[183] When called to emergencies, there was often insufficient time to put on his artificial leg, but he managed to provide anaesthesia and assist at operations using his crutches. He was on duty continuously for a week before he managed even a few hours leave.[184] By the time the epidemic had finally run its course at the end of 1919, 40 per cent of the Australian public had been infected and 15 000 had died.

While Roy was doing his residency at Sydney Hospital, he met a capable physician with an interest in neurosis and approached him about his 'difficulties'. Roy was advised to undertake psychoanalysis.

Psychoanalysis is the body of thought which brings the ideas of Sigmund Freud into a coherent theory. Unlike psychology, which focuses on the conscious world and aspects of socialisation, psychoanalysis privileges the life of the unconscious as the way to understand the psychic life.[185] Psychoanalysis was part of a general intellectual shift from a 19th century focus on learning by observing and documenting

---

181 Winn RC *Men May Rise* p197
182 Winn RC *Men May Rise* p198
183 Winn RC *Men May Rise* p216
184 Winn RC *Men May Rise* p216
185 Damousi J *Freud in the Antipodes* 2005 p1

the external world, to a new approach that used talking and listening to discover the inner world.[186]

Prior to 1914, Freud's ideas were not in common currency in Australia and were little known outside medical circles.[187] Although Freud, Jung and Havelock Ellis were invited to read papers at the Australian Medical Congress as early as 1911, the medical fraternity remained unconvinced and continued to stress physical factors in treating mental conditions.[188] Nonetheless, there were some medical men, like the unidentified physician Roy approached at Sydney Hospital, who saw value in the new ideas of the mind.

It is likely that Freud's theories for treating shell shock, as well as Roy's own desire to have treatment for his depression and jealousy, sparked his consideration of psychoanalysis. However, as it was not available in Australia, he would have to seek treatment in London or New York.[189] Roy chose London, where he could further his medical studies at the same time. He was open to learning about modern methods for treating mental disorders and started preparing himself by reading textbooks and making contacts in Britain. Roy's 1919 diary records the name and address of Ernest Jones – one of the key figures in the British psychoanalytical firmament and a man with whom Roy would have a long-standing relationship.[190]

---

186 Damousi J *Freud in the Antipodes* 2005 p4
187 Damousi J *Freud in the Antipodes* 2005 p27
188 Damousi J *Freud in the Antipodes* 2005 p28
189 Winn RC *Men May Rise* p217
190 Winn RC *Diary 16 September 1919*

THE CONTINUAL INNER SEARCH

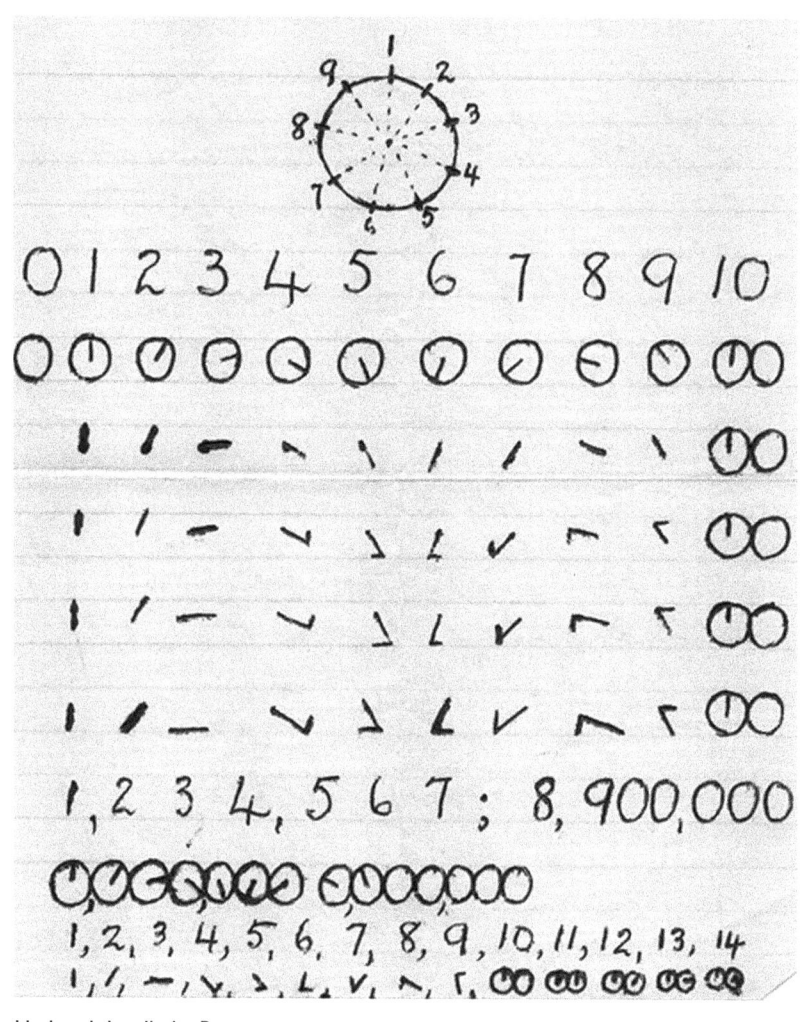

Undated doodle by Roy

5

Psychoanalytical Treatment in the UK

In January 1920, after completing his residency at Sydney Hospital, Roy, Bertha and their year-old baby Betty, travelled to Britain via Honolulu and Canada. Roy recorded the costs per person of each leg of the journey – £32 for a 2nd class berth to San Francisco, £20 for rail to New York and £25 pounds for 2nd class berth to Liverpool.[191]

In London, Roy undertook postgraduate studies with special attention to neurology at University College, London, and the Maudsley Neurological Hospital. At University College he studied the anatomy of the nervous system and attended a course on physiology. At Maudsley, he worked in the laboratory and attended the preliminary course for the Diploma of Psychological Medicine but for some unknown reason did not go on to sit for the examination.

As well as studying, he also worked for the Medical Re-survey Boards at the Ministry of Pensions from August 1920 to November 1921. He had resident appointments at West London Hospital in 1921, the year their son Richard William (Dick) was born; and at North Middlesex Hospital in 1922, where he was in charge of a children's ward of 30 beds and several adult medical wards. At North Middlesex, he 'distinguished himself highly in his work. He proved a very gentlemanly colleague'.[192]

---

191 Winn RC *Diary 16 September 1919*
192 Mort S *Reference for Roy Winn* North Middlesex Hospital 28 March 1923

Although the year is uncertain, a letter dated 22 May from Ernest Jones inviting Roy to lunch at his home in Sussex, suggests that Roy was also actively forging relationships with lynchpins in the psychoanalytical world.

From July 1920 to July 1922, Roy undertook psychoanalysis with Dr Robert Marmaduke Riggall of the British Psychoanalytical Society.[193] Riggall was only nine years older than Roy but, from the beginning, Roy had a favourable opinion of him, finding his quiet manner and unblustering confidence reassuring.[194]

Riggall was the medical director of Northumberland House, a private psychiatric nursing home in Finchley committed to personalised and humane treatment of mental disorders. He was also interested in some of the emerging disciplines like anthropology that, in the 1920s, were expanding the intellectual horizon. He wrote a book review of Bronislaw Malinowski's groundbreaking work in the Trobriand Islands and articles on art and laughter.

At the first consultation, Riggall asked Roy numerous questions but, unlike at a usual medical consultation, he did not perform a physical examination. According to Roy's novel, this 'no touch' approach was standard psychoanalytical practice as, if the patient thought there was anything physically wrong, he should not be attending for psychoanalysis.

The next day, Roy was asked to lie on a couch, which was placed to face away from Riggall, who explained that Roy was expected to say anything that came to his mind. Roy talked without difficulty and was glad he had found someone who was not bored by having to listen to his problems. Weeks went by in this way, with lots of talk and occasional silences.

Thus Roy started to have some insight into his own mind and began to apply his newfound power to understanding the behaviour

---

193 Robert Riggall 1881–1970
194 Winn RC *Men May Rise* p226

of others. He came to realise that his symptoms were not as unusual as he had thought. Although in one way he prided himself on being different from other people, in another he was relieved to find himself not as unusual as he had imagined.[195] He acquired respect for the ordinary man, the individual who rarely runs to extremes. He came to realise that psychoanalysis has the effect of emphasising friendliness and humanity rather than wit and spurious cleverness.[196]

As the months passed, he acquired a more natural attitude to sex. He remembered how his mother used to say 'shocks' when he ran around naked as a young boy and he began to think of a healthy body as something to be admired rather than condemned. Sex became less a thing of stealth and shamefacedness and was to be enjoyed. As the wish to enjoy life found expression, he also acquired the wish to work.[197]

Every month that passed showed an improvement in his condition. He was less jealous and could contemplate with equanimity Bertha showing an ordinary interest in the other men she met. His insomnia lessened. He could finally sleep.[198]

But it was not to last. As predicted by Dr Riggall, he entered the negative phase of analysis. He developed a vague fear of, and hostile feelings towards Riggall. He missed appointments and he made excuses. The old symptoms returned with greater severity and new symptoms surfaced. He found it increasingly difficult to continue at work. The responsibility of it played on his mind. He feared that he might poison his patients by prescribing too big a dose of medicine or that his hand might slip when he was doing routine surgical treatment.[199] He could not handle knives without feelings of dread and he had to stop working as a surgeon. One day he was appalled by the thought of attacking Bertha with a knife; on another he stormed at Riggall and threatened to kill him. He thought he was going mad. If it had not been for the

---

195 Winn RC *Men May Rise* p226
196 Winn RC *Men May Rise* p226
197 Winn RC *Men May Rise* p226
198 Winn RC *Men May Rise* p228
199 Winn RC *Men May Rise* p238

understanding attitude of his analyst he could not have carried on.[200]

This was also a very hard time for Bertha. She suffered because of the return of his insomnia and because she was again accused of preferring other men. She had to put up with Roy's moods and his cynical outbursts against her heart-felt beliefs, including calling religious people 'hypocrites' and decrying all religion as 'nonsense'.[201]

Finally, after two years, Roy's analysis came to an end and Riggall shook his hand, the only time he did so.[202] Roy had made good progress and could now look into his own psyche with detachment and a balanced attitude.[203] He had become a convert to psychoanalysis and believed that it was the only thing that could make men free. There was no real education in life without it.[204] He was to devote the rest of his life to psychoanalysis and the exploration of his own and other people's minds. On Roy's return to Australia, he kept in regular touch with Riggall, including when Riggall visited Australia in 1934. He also kept up with his other British psychoanalytical contacts like Ernest Jones.

In early 1921, Roy had written a long letter to his parents about Dick's birth and Bertha's consequent radiance, which had dispelled her earlier apprehensive mood. The letter finishes with thanks for the cabling of £100 and a confession that, although he is reducing his expenditure somewhat, it takes some doing getting into proper habits, after always being accustomed to no habits at all. He says 'my tendency to extravagance[205] is being brought into focus with other things needing correction' and 'I am hardly able to recognize myself as the same man

---

200 Winn RC *Men May Rise* p238
201 Winn RC *Men May Rise* p239
202 Winn RC *Men May Rise* p251
203 Winn RC *Men May Rise* p251
204 Winn RC *Men May Rise* p261
205 Winn RC *Diary 16 September 1919* records that he bought Bertha a purse for £15 at a time when a first-class berth across the Pacific was £47.

who left Australia in 1920'.[206] It is not clear whether these comments relate to managing money, his mental state, or both.

Ellen Hurford: always called Nanny

The family returned to Sydney on the SS *Ormonde* in September 1922, bringing with them Ellen Hurford as nanny to Betty and baby Dick who was now 19 months old. Nanny lived with the family, raising all the children until they left home, when she transitioned to the post of general housekeeper. She retired to Goolwa in South Australia to be with her sister in the 1960s and died in 1981. She was always an integral, much loved part of the family.

---

206 Winn RC *Letter to William and Janet Winn* 27 February 1921

Sydney Hospital medical staff 1924: Roy (back, third left)

6

Committing to the Inner Search

Once back in Australia Roy entered general practice at his house at 83 Birriga Road, Bellevue Hill. He was also appointed Honorary Relieving Assistant Physician at Sydney Hospital in 1924, and then Honorary Assistant Physician in 1926. He often came home smelling of anaesthetic ether – but at least it was a change from the smell of stale cigarettes from his chain-smoking. At Sydney Hospital, he developed an interest in diabetes, wrote a paper on it[207] and was one of the first to give insulin injections, saving many lives. He wrote a paper on the psychogalvanometer,[208] a machine which some, including Roy, argued could indicate certain emotions.[209] He also worked as medical officer at the Newtown Baby Health Centre.

In 1930 Roy applied for a position as a physician at the Coast Hospital,[210] an infectious diseases establishment. He did not get the job, despite the fact that he listed at least a dozen names of eminent British physicians with whom he had contact.[211]

---

207 Winn RC *Simplification of the Dietetic Treatment of Diabetes Mellitus* undated
208 Winn RC 'The Psychogalvanometer in Practice' *Australasian Journal of Psychology and Philosophy 1929*. The psychogalvanometer was an instrument for testing mental reaction, by determining how skin resistance changes when a voltage is applied to electrodes in contact with the skin.
209 https://freudinoceania.com/2012/08/11/the-psychogalvanometer-can-emotions-be-measured/
210 Coast Hospital was called Prince Henry Hospital from 1934
211 Winn RC *Draft application for appointment to the Coast Hospital* 19 July 1930

The Coast application provides an interesting insight into the seeming importance of connections with the great and good of the British medical fraternity in gaining Australian medical positions, although in this case it did not succeed. It also introduces some of the key international players in the medical world of the mind; men with whom Roy is likely to have continued a correspondence after his return to Australia, including Dr William McDougall, Professor of Psychology at Harvard; Dr Ely Gellife; Sir Frederick Mott and Dr Frederick Golla from the Maudsley Hospital; and the neurologist Dr Grainge Stewart.

Although Roy was developing a deep interest in neurosis, it was leavened at times by a light-hearted approach to life. He valued nonsense and often mixed it with medical themes and classics. His poem *Lists of Slips in Diagnosis* below was inspired by Homer's catalogue of ships and framed through the lens of medicine, his own humorous bent and his amputation. The layperson certainly needs a medical dictionary to begin to understand it and perhaps only fellow medical practitioners can really appreciate its cleverness.

> Agromegaly, Neurasthenia
> Agonising Mumps
> Hepatomegaly, Psychasthenia
> And cephalic bumps.
>
> Melancholic, Intussusception
> Phantom pains in stumps
> Unpoetic things to mention
> Sundry faecal lumps.
>
> Pyelonephritis and Cystitis
> Sediments in the sumps
> Stricturing and Balanitis
> Troubles with the pumps.
>
> Photophobia, Obstipation
> Patients in the dumps
> Sundry lacks in consolation

Suffered by the frumps.

Extremely widespread inflammation
Patients with the humps
Concentrated vituperation
Yells from surging clumps.

In 1931, Roy decided to open his own private practice as a full-time psychoanalyst. He sold the family home in Bellevue Hill in order to buy consulting rooms in the Harley Building, 143 Macquarie Street Sydney and, with the phone number B 2156, opened for business.

Roy believed passionately that, as psychoanalysis had helped him, so it could help others whose current treatments were proving ineffective.[212] He was particularly interested in the impact of war on soldiers and sought to find a treatment that aimed at 'relieving deeply buried emotions, such as guilt concerning the impulse to kill'.[213]

The social and cultural historian, Joy Damousi, says that Roy was 'the first trained psychoanalyst to practise in Australia'.[214] He certainly was the first to practice full-time but, at this point, he had apparently received no formal training and his only personal exposure to the method had been as a patient. Given that Roy believed passionately in psychoanalysis and that he was not the sort of person to embark upon something lightly, one must assume that he was reading all the available psychoanalytical literature, and communicating with, and learning from, its European and British practitioners. Peter Ellingsen, a former journalist who became a psychotherapist, and who wrote a history of psychoanalysis in Australia, reports that Roy had been in correspondence with Freud from the first decades of the 20th century.[215]

Psychoanalytical practice at that time in Australia was a risky proposition for a number of reasons. Psychoanalysis was unlikely to pay well.

---

212 Winn RW *Memoirs of Richard (Dick) Winn* 2003 p6
213 Winn RC *Psychoanalysis in Wartime,* Australian Nurses Journal Vol. 15 January 1943 p4
214 Damousi J *Freud in the Antipodes* 2005 p33
215 Ellingsen P *A History of Psychoanalysis in Australia* 2013 p89

Patients had one-hour sessions at least three times a week and few could afford such expense. Dick said that Roy was not at all interested in money and would still see patients who could not afford the fees. This was confirmed by Reg Martin, a future psychoanalytical colleague, who indicated that Roy was fortunate to have sufficient funds from his stake in Winn's Ltd that he did not have to rely solely on his professional earnings.[216] Still, finances would have been tight, especially during the early 1930s, years of the Great Depression.

As he was the first person in Australia to practise psychoanalysis full-time, there was no precedent and no certainty of success. He was pursuing an unpopular career, which would be lived out in a cold and hostile professional climate.[217] There was much negativity from the medical establishment and antagonism from psychiatrists. Many friends and acquaintances from the social circles in which Roy and his family moved also frowned upon psychoanalysis, judging it as radical and perverted.

After writing an article for the *Medical Journal of Australia* in 1936, the journal published a letter in response that claimed 'the theory of infantile sexuality was the greatest libel that has ever been published about the human race …' and that 'the greatest argument against the Freudian doctrine lies in the fact that it has been so readily accepted and practised by charlatans and unqualified persons'.[218]

It is no wonder that when Roy offered to treat public patients from Sydney Hospital free at his new consulting rooms, the hospital board turned down his offer on the grounds it could not be party to acknowledging psychoanalysis.[219] [220] Nevertheless, like the second Australian analyst, Melbourne-based Paul Dane, Roy got used to looks of lofty disdain on the faces of his medical colleagues.[221] In 1934 he resigned

---

216 Martin R *Speech for Inauguration of the Winn Library* 1993
217 Nield J *Speech to commemorate Roy Winn's death* 1974
218 McGeorge J *Correspondence MJA* 14 March 1936
219 Martin R *Speech for the Inauguration of the Winn Library* 1993
220 It may also have been because of hospital concerns about psychoanalysis constituting an 'exclusive dogma' and thus being in contravention of the BMA Code of Ethics.
221 Ellingsen P *A History of Psychoanalysis in Australia* 2013 p92

his Honorary Assistant Physician position at Sydney Hospital citing pressure of psychoanalytical work.[222]

It was not only colleagues who disapproved. Dick believed that Bertha found Roy's decision to practice psychoanalysis very difficult and would have preferred that he continue as a general medicine doctor. Notwithstanding, she appears to have supported Roy and never, to Dick's knowledge, ever publicly criticised the decision.

After a slow start, Roy appears to have had a steady stream of private patients. Understandably, I have no access to files on these patients, the reasons for their attendance or their progress. The only information I have is that one patient was a medical man with symptoms of paranoia.[223] Dick recalled that Roy had told him that he had treated a number of homosexual scoutmasters who had sought him out to be 'cured', unsuccessfully. As a consequence, Roy did not want his boys to join the Boy Scouts where he thought they might be exposed to unwanted attentions.

In the early days of his Harley Building practice, Roy was exercised by concerns about the privacy of his patients. The design of the building, with a number of doctors working on each floor from a central corridor, plus the hourly back-to-back psychoanalytical sessions, meant it was difficult to minimise the chance of patients seeing each other. Although Roy shared a door attendant with a dentist on his floor, she could not be expected to prevent inadvertent meetings in the corridor. He wrote to Ernest Jones of the International Psychoanalytical Society asking his advice about whether, like the Austrian-British psychoanalyst Melanie Klein, it was justifiable to make his sessions 50 minutes rather than an hour in order to reduce 'the dissipation of transference, or would this be less important than loss of time?'[224] Unfortunately, Roy's papers do not include any response from Jones.

Roy was interested in all fields related to human behavior and the

---

222   Winn RC *Letter to Sydney Hospital* 24 June 1934
223   Winn RC *Letter to Ernest Jones* 22 October 1935
224   Winn RC *Letter to Ernest Jones* 22 October 1935

mind, as attested by his membership of the Australian Association of Psychology and Philosophy and the Australian Anthropological Society. For Roy, psychoanalysis was understood through the forgotten primitive language of symbolism.[225] He was fascinated by the use of the consonant M in the name for 'mother' in the world's languages,[226] and was exploring connections with anthropologist Margaret Mead while she was touring Australia.[227]

He joined the Royal Australian Historical Society and was especially interested in the history of mental illness and its measurement. He had a large notebook in which he summarised all the unproved and discredited methods of measuring mental illness from palmistry through phrenology to handwriting; the luminaries who developed modern mental testing from the English pioneer Francis Galton, through the French psychologist Alfred Binet, to the tests used by the US Army; the beginnings of vocational guidance; personality tests; IQ tests and the definitions of measurement terms such as the decile curve, validity and correlation.

Roy continued to be an open-minded and lateral thinker and did not always follow the orthodox psychoanalytical line. Sigmund Freud, in the first known letter to an Australian analyst, declined Roy's invitation to write a preface to a book that Roy was planning in 1931. Roy's book aimed to link Freud's discoveries with the stimulus-reflex findings of Ivan Pavlov.

Pavlov had found that objects or events could trigger a conditioned response. In his famous experiments with dogs, he could provoke a salivary response simply by pressing a buzzer. Roy appears to have been interested in expanding this work and exploring behavioural responses to mental triggers. However, in later life Freud became increasingly preoccupied with what he saw as the watering down of

---

225   Damousi J *Freud in the Antipodes* 2005 p66
226   Baker S *Letter to Roy Winn* 11 February 1946
227   Godwin E *Letter to Roy Winn* 20 July 1951

his methodology[228] and he told Roy that he objected to the introduction of Pavlov's experiments into psychoanalytical theory.

Although Freud thought it dangerous to change the psychological viewpoint for the physiological one, Roy continued to pursue the idea for 20 years and, even though he considered Freud a genius,[229] he was unswayed by some of the genius's views. As late as 1952, he gave a paper in Melbourne, 'Interrelations between the Development of Speech and Locomotion' where he portrayed speech as a Pavlovian correlate of behaviour.[230] To classical Freudians, the widespread public and professional conflation of physiology and psychology with psychoanalysis was regrettable. This example of Roy steadfastly following his own line of thought is typical of the man I remember. Roy was never one to be pressured to change his position just because he was challenged by a more powerful contradictory doctrine.

From the 1930s onwards the psychoanalytical world had been loosening into various theoretical schools, and arguments about their respective merits were heart-felt. As elsewhere, Australia had psychoanalysts who were influenced by the Hungarian psychoanalyst Sandor Ferenczi,[231] others who favoured Melanie Klein, and still others that looked to Frenchman Jacques Lacan. Roy does not seem to have been willing to tie his colours to any one mast. During the early 1920s he had rejected the shackles of religious doctrine; he was not now going to adopt any new restraints on his thinking and practice. He wanted to take any useful idea from wherever it came. For those who wanted to keep psychoanalysis pure, his eclectic, cherry-picking approach was not always appreciated.

In 1952, Betty Joseph, a specialist in child analysis in the British Psychoanalytical Society and an influential member of the London psychoanalytical fraternity, wrote to Roy about a paper he had written, 'Mental Development'. Roy had sent the paper to Melanie Klein, who

---

228 Damousi J *Freud in the Antipodes* 2005 p80
229 Winn RC *Psychoanalysis and General Practice* MJA 29 February 1936
230 Ellingsen P *A History of Psychoanalysis in Australia* 2013 p137
231 Clara Lazar-Geroe leaned towards Ferenczi, Reg Martin towards Klein

also had an interest in children, and she had passed it on to Joseph for comment. Betty Joseph said she had real difficulties with the paper as Roy was using analytical concepts, while the ideas behind them were far removed from psychoanalytical work.[232] Roy responded to her by saying he hoped that she was mistaken and that his speculations might prove to be of benefit. He then wrote a long exposition of his argument. Roy was not one to throw in the towel if he believed in something strongly enough.

There are only two extant letters from Freud in the Winn archive. The first is Freud's aforementioned 1931 letter, written in English on Bergasse 19 Wien letterhead. It starts warmly 'I have been much interested in the rich content of your letter. I hope you will be able to fulfill your intention of publishing…' The letter is signed 'with kind regards, Freud'.

In 1958 Roy made a note on a copy of this letter from Freud. He says he was glad that he had had enough sense to destroy the proposed manuscript in question but defends himself by saying that there was only a passing reference to conditioned reflexes in it. He goes further and says that his manuscript posited the idea of two classes of marriage – a minor class and a major. The first would be a registered trial marriage without the birth of any children, the second would be a marriage for which there should be no divorce unless it was to the advantage of the children. Whether the idea is good or bad doesn't concern him but Freud's letter decided him to confine his interest to the scientific rather than the cultural.[233]

Roy wrote again to Freud in 1933 suggesting that Freud should write an intimate autobiography. Interestingly, this time Freud's reply was in German and the tone is weary. Freud notes that Roy remains an enthusiast who feels very much more certain about the future than he does. He says that Roy's wish for him to write an autobiography

---

232   Joseph B *Letter to Roy Winn* London 21 March 1952
233   Winn RC Note on back of copy of *Sigmund Freud's letter to Roy Winn* 25 October 1931

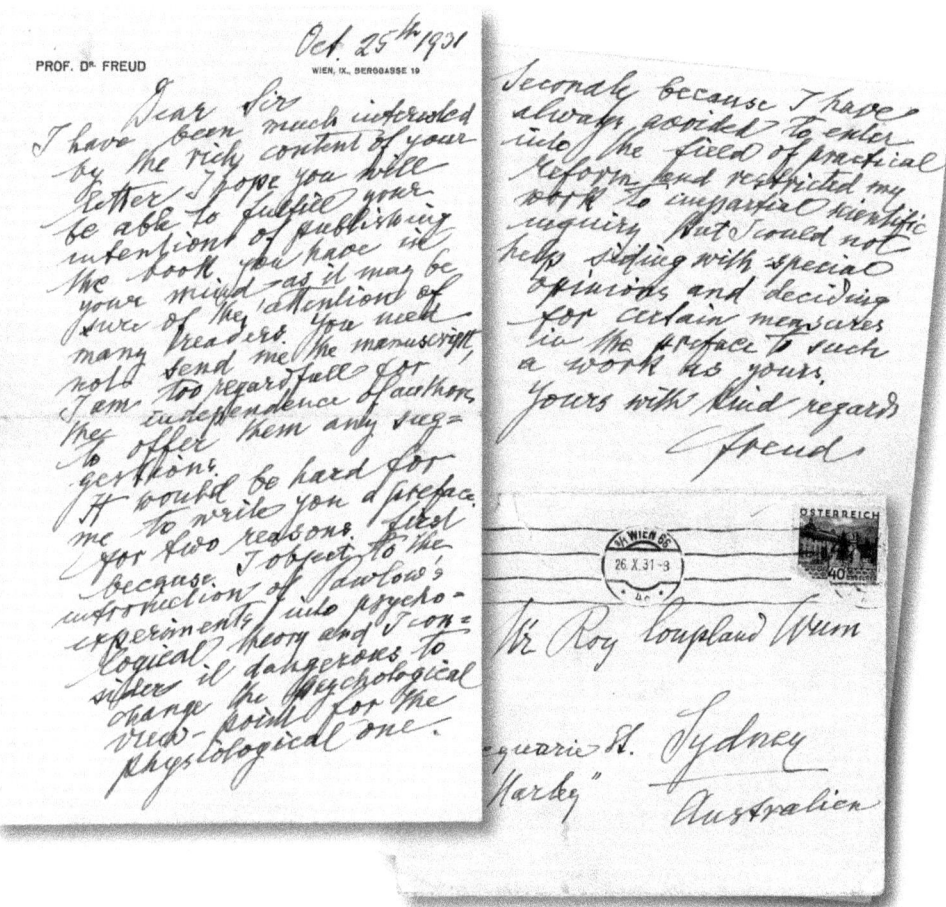

Sigmund Freud's 1931 letter to Roy

will remain unfulfilled. The amount of exhibitionism, which his 1899 book about the unconscious, *Interpretation of Dreams*, has demanded of him, is burdensome and all he demands personally from the world is to be left in peace, while giving attention to psychoanalysis. It is signed 'with very friendly greetings, yours, Freud'.

Roy's undated note on this 1933 letter says that, although he still thinks it is a pity that Freud turned down his suggestion about an autobiography, he recognises that Freud would have received more 'bricks than bouquets' if he had proceeded. Roy goes on to say that, in his opinion, it will be a very long time before the general principles of psychoanalysis influence the science of psychology.

Roy promoted the view that psychoanalysis should only be expounded by the well-trained.[234] However, there were some who felt that Roy himself was not adequately trained. Peter Ellingsen claims that Roy and Paul Dane[235] practised a faltering and inexpert version of the Freudian method.[236] Ellingsen goes further and states that Roy's credentials were shaky and his competence doubted by his own analyst and to those to whom he turned for recognition.[237] I don't know what evidence Ellingsen had for his view but Roy's acceptance as an associate member of the British Psychoanalytical Society in 1935 was personally supported by both Robert Riggall, his former analyst, and Ernest Jones of the International Psychoanalytical Association, neither of whom had any reason to support a candidate of doubtful competence on the far side of the world.[238]

Joy Damousi said Roy became a member of the British Psychoanalytical Society while in London but I do not think this was the case.[239] After receiving notification by cablegram, Roy wrote to Jones from Australia, saying how pleased he was to have been accepted for membership. He was to remain an associate, not a full member of the society, for 15 years.

In 1938 Roy alerted Paul Dane that Ernest Jones from the International Psychoanalytical Association was desperately seeking emigration for many European analysts following Nazi Germany's annexation of Austria. Jones found the new head of immigration at Australia House

---

234 Ellingsen P *A History of Psychoanalysis in Australia* 2013 p75
235 Paul Dane from Melbourne was the second fulltime practising analyst in Australia
236 Ellingsen P *A History of Psychoanalysis in Australia* 2013 p71
237 Ellingsen P *A History of Psychoanalysis in Australia* 2013 p87
238 Winn RC *Letter to Ernest Jones* 22 October 1935
239 Damousi J *Freud in the Antipodes* 2005 p49

in London ill-educated and unsympathetic to the cause.[240] Roy worked with Dane and other supportive doctors and influential people to help persuade the relevant Australian departments to accept applications from six European training analysts. However, disappointingly, of the six, only Dr Clara Lazar-Geroe from Hungary was supported to emigrate, arriving in Melbourne in 1940 to become Australia's first training analyst.[241] When Lazar-Geroe began psychoanalytical training activities at the newly founded Melbourne Institute for Psychoanalysis, Roy lent enthusiastic support and joined the foundation board in 1941.

Roy was also keen to develop a small group in Sydney and, as early as 1939, wrote to Robert Riggall about a number of people arriving in Sydney who were interested in psychoanalysis. Ernest Jones, who was shown the letter by Riggall, understood Roy's desire to have a group of practising analysts who could form the nucleus of a society in Sydney but cautioned about the need for them to be trained before they practised psychoanalysis. In early 1942 Roy wrote to Jones who reiterated his support of the idea of a Sydney group and held out the carrot of ultimate affiliation with the British Psychoanalytical Society, provided it was restricted to really serious workers.[242] Jones mentioned that he had been approached in a similar vein by the Australian Psychological Centre, about whose 40-strong members he knew nothing. Roy responded six months later that he did not recognise the centre but had formed a small group comprising himself, Clara Lazar-Geroe and Dr Siegfried Fink, who had fled to Australia from Switzerland in 1938.

By the early 1950s, Clara Lazar-Geroe was exercised by both Roy's and Paul Dane's failure to the meet the standards for full membership of the British Psychoanalytical Society, especially the requirement of presentation of adequate case histories. Essentially, Clara was torn

---

240 Jones E *Letter from International Psychoanalytical Association to Roy Winn* 5 July 1939
241 Chapman C *Inner Worlds, Portraits and Psychology* National Portrait Gallery 2011 p125 and 159
242 Jones E *Letter to Roy Winn* 9 January 1942

between guarding the integrity of a young organisation by disallowing insufficiently trained members on the one hand, and avoiding hurting the feelings of those who had pioneered the work on the other. Clara thought Roy would feel it very acutely if he could not become a full member and considered that his great personal integrity offset, to a great extent, his case-study shortcomings.[243]

In 1950 Dr Andrew Peto, who was also from Hungary, asked the British Psychoanalytical Society's Training Committee to make an exception in favour of Roy. In 1951, the society changed its rules so that Roy could be accredited without giving the necessary case histories, and both Roy and Paul Dane became full members of both the British Psychoanalytical Society and the London Institute of Psychoanalysis.[244]

That same year, Roy made a generous endowment towards the establishment of a second Australian psychoanalytical training institute, this time in Sydney. Premises were eventually purchased in the 1980s, at 5 Penshurst St. Ellingsen suggests[245] that Roy may have endowed the Sydney Institute for Psychoanalysis as a way of gaining full membership, but that does not accord with Dick's or indeed my own knowledge of Roy, and according to his colleague Reg Martin, its establishment was solely because of Roy's enthusiasm and interest in analysis. The inaugural board included Roy, Andrew Peto and Siegfried Fink, as well as Clara Lazar-Geroe. Dr Peto, distinguished internationally, , was engaged as its first training analyst.

Persuading Andrew Peto to settle in Sydney was, for Roy, a two-fold achievement of great importance. First, it enabled his long-cherished hope that analysts could be trained in Sydney to become a reality. Second, it opened the possibility that he could have additional personal analysis and thereby eventually become a training analyst himself.

According to Janet Nield, his friend and fellow analyst, Roy had

---

243 Ellingsen P *A History of Psychoanalysis in Australia* 2013 p103
244 Ellingsen P *A History of Psychoanalysis in Australia* 2013 p103
245 Ellingsen P *A History of Psychoanalysis in Australia* 2013 p103

been dissatisfied with the depth of his own analysis and, to her knowledge, on two occasions submitted to further analysis. He could have pretended that such an extension of insight was too dangerous for one of his age or that, as the doyen of his country, he had no further need to subject himself to the pain of new revelations, but he didn't.[246] He appears always to have been keen to extend his knowledge and broaden his perspective – to really understand himself.

Roy revealed his insight and critical judgment in personal and private discussion. He was 'not afraid to voice his irrational untried opinions or hunches but was much more ruthless than the prejudiced in scrutinising their origin and durability'.[247] He could be angry and attacking yet he was never malicious or wounding to others. He was humble and dignified, wise and brave, but he forgave himself and his associates when they fell short of the ideal.[248]

Despite repeated attempts, Andrew Peto failed to have his medical qualifications recognised in NSW and left Sydney for an appointment in New York in 1955. Roy's hopes for continued training were dashed but he tenaciously held the Sydney Institute for Psychoanalysis together, hoping that training in Sydney would eventually become a reality.[249]

For Roy, an important aim of the society was to forge connections within the professional psychiatric community and to broaden its support. In the *Medical Journal of Australia* Roy outlined the ambitious aims of the fledgling institute: 'conduct courses of study for psychiatrists and other medical graduates, to foster research, to found a library, to start a child guidance clinic, to study group therapy, and to pursue the traditional psychoanalytical interest in anthropology, education, sociology and psychometrics. In short, to make psychoanalysis more readily available to the general community'.[250] These ambitious aims

---

246 Nield J *Speech to commemorate Roy Winn's death* 1974
247 Nield J *Speech to commemorate Roy Winn's death* 1974
248 Nield J *Speech to commemorate Roy Winn's death* 1974
249 Martin R *Speech for Inauguration of SIP's Winn Library* 1993
250 Winn RC *Medical Societies* MJA 7 July 1951 p26 cited in Chapman C *Inner Worlds, Portraits and Psychology* National Portrait Gallery 2011 p125

confirm Roy's wide interests and his desire to make analysis available to as many people as possible.

Roy played a very active role in the affairs and expansion of the Sydney Institute for Psychoanalysis during its first decade. He appears to have overseen and paid for its initial legal formation and served as its chair, at least once in 1955. In 1952, Roy and Andrew Peto joined Clara Lazar-Geroe's initiative to form the Australian Psychoanalytical Society as a branch of the British Psychoanalytical Society. In 1967, it became independent and, in 1973, a full member of the International Psychoanalytical Association.

The Sydney institute still operates from the Willoughby premises, to which Roy bequeathed over 20 psychoanalytical books including those by Klein, Freud, Ernest Jones, Geza Roheim,[251] Abraham Brill[252] and John Flugel,[253] as well as articles, journals and notebooks on his cases, and four volumes of Freud's collected papers. The journals reportedly have thoughtful comments and annotations in the margins – exhibiting Roy's dedication and passion for his subject on every page. There is a photographic portrait of Roy on the wall, although a current analyst I met during a visit did not know who it portrayed or why it was there.

In 1993 the Sydney institute dedicated its library as the Roy Winn Library and in the last few years opened the Winn Clinic, an online portal to enable members of the public access to psychoanalytical practitioners. It is training psychoanalysts in China and supporting psychoanalytical work in Taiwan and Korea. I am sure that Roy would be gratified to know that the Sydney Institute for Psychoanalysis had not only survived into the new century but was supporting analysts all over the region.

I have had little access to information about Roy's general psychoanalytical views and have had to rely on his journal publications and

---

251 Hungarian psychologist and anthropologist
252 Austrian-American psychiatrist and early translator of Freud's works into English
253 British psychoanalyst whose works include the psychology of clothes

conference papers to build a picture of his thinking. From the beginning to the end of his career, he regularly attended and presented papers at state and national psychiatric and psychoanalytical meetings and conferences. He was less keen on preparing scientific papers for official journals or for wider publication.

The papers for psychoanalytical meetings range from those on the theories of Melanie Klein and psychoanalytical technique at the first psychoanalytical conference in Australia, in Melbourne in 1946, to a paper on manic depression in Adelaide in 1955.

Roy saw psychoanalysis sitting within the medical model and believed that it was dependent on general medical acceptance for its advancement.[254] To this end, he remained a member of the Australian Medical Association and was committed to educating medical practitioners about all facets of psychoanalysis, always hoping to bridge the gulf between it and medicine. He was one of the foundation members of the Australasian Association of Psychiatrists in 1946, regularly attending its meetings and pressing his case.

To reach the wider general medical fraternity, Roy wrote four major articles for the *Medical Journal of Australia*. The first was 'Psychoanalysis and General Practice' in February 1936,[255] the second 'Contributions of Psycho-Analysis to General Medicine' in March 1936,[256] followed by 'Psychoanalysis and Allied Forms of Therapy' in 1940[257] and the revised 'Psychoanalysis and other Forms of Psychotherapy' in May 1948.[258]

'Psychoanalysis and General Practice' aims to provide an understanding of the causes of psychogenic illnesses and promotes psychoanalysis as the best instrument available for their treatment. The paper starts lyrically: 'Though poets in every age have dimly recognised the hidden depths of the human mind, Freud was the first to

---

254 Ellingsen P*A History of Psychoanalysis in Australia* 2013 p90
255 Winn RC 'Psychoanalysis and General Practice' *MJA* 29 February 1936 p293
256 Winn RC 'Contributions of Psychoanalysis to General Medicine' *MJA* 7 March 1936 p329
257 Winn RC 'Psycho-Analysis and Allied Forms of Psychotherapy' *MJA* November 1940
258 Winn RC 'Psycho-Analysis and other Forms of Psychotherapy' *MJA* May 1948

demonstrate scientifically that what we call thinking is not synonymous with consciousness, but includes processes which are entirely unconscious'.[259] The paper gives a useful analogy of a volcano for the relationship between conscious and unconscious mental processes, likening the powerful forces deep below the surface to the unconscious impulses.[260]

The use of metaphor is considered a useful bridge to help try to bring others on board, making them aware of what they already knew in their hearts.[261] However, if this paper's aim was to use a volcanic metaphor to bridge the gulf between analysts and the rest of the medical profession, its language and tone do nothing to assist. It pulls no punches in its criticism of academic psychologists who once asserted the non-existence of the unconscious and still ignore powerful unconscious mental urges. It lauds Freud as a genius and lambasts those, like Carl Jung and Alfred Adler, who Roy felt were lesser men succumbing to mental blindness about Freud's most important discoveries.

The second paper, 'Contributions of Psycho-Analysis to General Medicine' draws on the work of Franz Alexander[262] who combined psychoanalytical treatment with physical examination of his patients who had additional alimentary, respiratory, convulsive, hypertensive, endocrine or infectious disorders. Alexander's work appears to align with Roy's previously mentioned interest in Pavlovian conditioned physiological responses. However, Alexander was not in favour and even as late as 1980s there was little encouragement for trainees to read him.[263]

One of Roy's general themes at this time was that analysis could treat physical as well as mental ailments, notably infectious disease. His line of argument was that the curative powers of psychoanalysis could enhance immunity to infection, but without offering any clinical

---

259 Winn RC 'Psychoanalysis and General Practice' *MJA* 29 February 1936 p293
260 Winn RC 'Psychoanalysis and General Practice' *MJA* 29 February 1936 p293
261 Sullivan, Leonie *personal communication* 2020
262 Franz Alexander was Professor of Psychoanalysis University of Chicago
263 Sullivan, Leonie *personal communication* 2020

research evidence to support his thesis, he was condemned by many in the medical profession.[264] Interestingly, although many questions remain about the operation of the immune system, modern medical research suggests that chronic stress can suppress the immune system and its ability to fight disease. Therefore, reducing stress, whether physical or emotional, may help prevent infections and other disorders. Perhaps Roy was not as far from the mark as his medical colleagues believed at the time.

The third paper, 'Psychoanalysis and Allied Forms of Therapy', is surprisingly poorly written but appears to be about Alfred Adler's psychotherapeutic methods. It commences with the rather untactful comment that Adler's general psychotherapeutic system, known as 'individual psychology', over-emphasises the facts already observed by Freud and evades their more profound significance. But 'nevertheless it lends itself by reason of its very superficiality to application in general medicine'.[265] Roy rather baldly launches into explanations of various psychoanalytical terms used by Adler such as 'Inferiority Complex'. He observes that the time-consuming nature of psychoanalysis has led many individuals to shorten the process by using hypnosis; narco-analysis; and therapeutic conversation. Roy did not agree with these shortcuts and believed that trained psychoanalysts should produce more complete and lasting results.[266] However, he conceded that, provided the emphasis is placed on reviving emotions as well as on increasing each patient's self-understanding, Adler's constitutes the best technique for a general practitioner to adopt and the most useful for widespread use in war.[267] Roy ends with a warning that if the Adlerian method is improperly used it may degenerate into little more than innocuous conversation.

The revised 1948 paper 'Psychoanalysis and other Forms of

---

264 Ellingsen P *A History of Psychoanalysis in Australia* 2013 p91
265 Winn RC 'Psychoanalysis and Allied Forms of Therapy' *MJA* November 1940 p510
266 Damousi J *Freud in the Antipodes* 2005 p169
267 Winn RC *Psychoanalysis and Allied Forms of Therapy* MJA November 1940 p511

Psychotherapy' is a long one. It aimed to outline the scientific complexity of psychoanalysis, and to argue that other forms of psychotherapy can possess palliative value, provided they do not worsen the unconscious difficulties of the patient. It described the training of analysts and explanations of Freudian terms such as 'free association', 'transference', 'projection'[268] and the 'unconscious', as well as sexual and genital responses.[269] The paper also presented Roy's unique perspective on some aspects of the Freudian psychoanalytical discipline. Contrary to the orthodox position that projection is in contrast to identification[270], he posited that both projection and introjection[271] were variants of identification, essentially just contrasting varieties of a similar mechanism.

Roy remained keen for other health professionals, not just doctors, to understand something about psychoanalysis and so wrote an article on 'Psychoanalysis in War-Time' for the *Australasian Nurses' Journal* in 1943. It lists the three commonest symptoms of psychoneurosis as worry, irritability and insomnia, which he regards as indicators of mental conflict. For soldiers in wartime, a typical mental conflict is that between fighting and running away but it is unlikely to produce definite symptoms unless the individual has been exposed to pronounced emotional disturbances during childhood. As mental conflict during childhood is usually more potent than the adult problem that re-arouses it, the bulk of therapeutic attention should be directed towards it – but only if undertaken by a trained analyst.[272]

In 1952, Roy gave a paper at the Melbourne Institute for Psychoanalysis on 'The Borderline Concept'. It was a modified version of a 1950 paper called 'Mental Development' because several of Roy's

---

268 Projection: where an individual attributes his/her own unacceptable feelings and wishes to someone else, therefore denying responsibility for those urges.
269 Winn RC 'Psychoanalysis and Other Forms of Therapy' *MJA* 8 May 1948 p588
270 Identification: where an individual assimilates an aspect, property or attribute of another and is thus transformed wholly or partially.
271 Introjection: a process by which an individual replicates the behaviours and attributes of others.
272 Winn RC " *The Australasian Nurses' Journal* 15 January 1943

opinions had changed following new observations. The paper focuses on speech and locomotion in children and looks at 224 patients including 'schizoids, paranoids, cyclothymoids, obsessoids and hysteroids' and presents three short case studies. Roy agreed with Melanie Klein's observations of Oedipal urges in early infancy and stated his view that 'infantile sexuality is oedipal, sado-masochistic phallic genitality, whereas adult sexuality is non-oedipal and non sado-masochistic'.[273]

In 1955, in a paper to the Association of Psychiatrists, Roy mentions his interest in the work of German psychoanalyst Max Stern who published a paper on the use of the free association method[274] with two of his patients. Roy spent hundreds of hours writing and rewriting the free association comments elicited and adopted a similar method with some of his own patients, inviting them to doodle or draw at home and then write whatever came to mind while away from him. In 1957, Roy attended a conference at the Melbourne Institute of Psychoanalysis. I do not know what contribution he made there but he found time to purchase a copy of Sophocles' plays. He was clearly still interested in the classics.

Even the year before his retirement, Roy was still writing papers. 'Are Allusive Sequences[275] "symbolic?"' was presented in 1960 at the interstate conference of the Australian Society of Psychoanalysts in Melbourne. In a fragment of a draft, he said that he put the question because he was unable to test whether they are symbolic through interpretation of them in the transference situation.[276] The reason for this was that he only noticed them when they were in written material, such as letters received from patients or in published psychoanalytical case reports.

As well as the specific psychoanalytical papers mentioned above, there are some undated papers about Roy's views on other

---

273   Winn RC *The Borderline Concept* 1952
274   Free association: where a person shares any thoughts or feelings that come to mind
275   Allusive sequences: suggestive rather than explicit, making links and raising possibilities.
276   Transference: a form of displacement, where a new object is substituted for the original.

psycho-medical subjects. Roy wrote a story called *Long Bacon* about a testy interaction between a wife and a waitress in a restaurant, with the wife unhappy about the tough steak she has been given and the insulting response to her request for another one. The title of the story comes from the husband's memory of the name 'long pig' that Pacific cannibals gave to their victims.

There are detailed notes on the back side of the story suggesting that Roy used the restaurant narrative as a vehicle for elaboration of his ideas about the origins of alimentary disturbances like colitis, chronic constipation and diarrhoea. He posits that 'colitis is the result of disturbance of the first anal phase and gastric disorder the result of inability to adequately surmount the oral phase. Chronic constipation then represents an advance on the other two alimentary illnesses, arising as it does at a later stage of development. During the oral phase the infant not only expresses its libidinal impulses by wanting to eat, but defends itself from danger by these cannibalistic phantasies…'[277] The notes are incomplete but hint at two things. The first is that he continued to be interested in Alexander's and Pavlov's physiological responses and the second, that he was exploring a new theme related to respiratory function, which in his view 'is utilised by psycho-neurotic patients in order to express unconscious impulses.'[278]

Among Roy's papers is an undated analysis of Shakespeare's play *Timon of Athens*, in keeping with his broad interests and love of literature. The paper is titled '*Timon of Athens* and Rorschach Tests'. Roy suggests that the play diagnoses Timon's manic behaviour and depression. Timon's rants reference ten animals, of which eight are quadruped and two are non-quadruped. Roy muses that the ten animals correspond to the ten animal responses found in Rorschach tests and that the non-quadruped animals symbolise Shakespeare before he could crawl.[279]

He did not limit himself to analysing plays. In a letter to fellow

---

277 Winn RC *Long Bacon* undated
278 Winn RC *Long Bacon* undated
279 Winn RC *Timon of Athens* paper undated

analyst Janet Nield, enclosing a psychoanalytical paper for her perusal, he scribbled the following joke in the margin. 'A lot of Pekes got into a tram carriage and when some St Bernards tried to get in there was no room, so they complained to the guard who said 'you should never try to get into a tram this time of day. Don't you know it's peke hour'.' Roy followed by saying 'I reckon that's a good joke'.[280] He then pointed out that the joke contained the Quadruped-Separation-Sequence with the St Bernards as the quadrupeds, the 'no room' signifying deprivation/separation and the guard the biped.[281]

There is another paper, again undated, but of a very different kind. 'Cultivating Optimism' is a plea to older people to preserve that freshness of spirit and hopefulness of outlook that characterise the young, and offers a recipe to achieve it. It is only a short paper but in keeping with Roy's wide reading, manages to make references to Dickens, Meredith and Bacon. It makes explicit that one of Roy's aims 'is to make and keep our outlook on life tolerant, clear and sympathetic, admitting and welcoming variety of interest and keeping clear of shallow and unworthy prejudices against people or things'.[282] The world of 2020 with its increasing polarisation, intolerance and pessimism might well benefit from adopting Roy's clearly and simply articulated optimism project.

After Roy retired from active psychoanalytical practice in 1961, his time was largely occupied with the study of the phenomenon of weaning and its relationship to the development of locomotion, a subject upon which he had many original ideas.[283] Unfortunately, I do not have any specific information about this retirement work but there is a whole humorous chapter on locomotion in Roy's *Ideography*, which features later in the chapter on Poems and Nonsense Verse.

---

280   Winn RC *Letter to Janet Nield* 1 December 1955
281   Winn RC *Letter to Janet Nield* 1 December 1955
282   Winn RC *Cultivated Optimism being a Confession of Ideals* undated
283   Graham F *Obituary of Roy Winn* MJA 1964 p333

Bertha and the children: Dick, baby Murray and Betty 1928

7

Family Life

Roy and Bertha lived at 83 Birriga Road, Bellevue Hill, at least until 1929, as attested by 16mm film footage taken by his brother Harold, which shows the wider Winn family in the front garden of a single-storey house on the tramline. Roy is smoking and Betty and Dick are doing cartwheels, while Jimmie the fox terrier is racing around the garden. Bertha is holding their third child, Murray Michael, born in 1927. As well as children playing in the garden, male fox terriers appear to be a feature of Winn family life for, in addition to Jimmie, there were Derrie and Monty.[284] Jimmie was a great fighter and was nearly killed after he attacked two Alsatians at once.

There was also lots of music. Bertha played the piano and all the family except Roy would have singsongs. Dick said that Roy was not interested in singing himself but his poem *A Song* suggests that, at least in later life, he greatly enjoyed music.

Bertha was very English. She thought Britain was the most important place on Earth, missed it acutely and always called it home. She was a very active person, bright and talkative and loved to lunch and shop. She did not like ants, mosquitoes or heat. She believed in God and Christianity and regularly went to church,[285] attending both St Michael's Church, Vaucluse, where Dick sang as a boy soprano in the

---

284   Derrie born 1936 and Monty born 1943
285   Winn Murray *personal communication* 2008

Beloved car and fox terrier

choir and St Mark's Anglican Church, Darling Point, where Roy's great friend, Canon Bader, presided. Along with most of her set, she was intolerant of Catholics. When her daughter showed a romantic interest in Catholic boy and 'go-getter' Jock Pagan, she gave Betty a ticket on an ocean liner bound for England to quash the romance – ultimately a successful strategy.[286]

Roy did not attend church or subscribe to any particular religion but towards the end of his life took a strong interest in, although never adopted, the universalist religious philosophy espoused at the newly-built Bahai Temple at Terrey Hills.[287]

Bertha believed in honesty, charity, hard work, thrift, cleanliness and good manners.[288] Roy subscribed to the same virtues, notwithstanding his struggles to practise thrift. He was friendly and kind, and

---

286 Winn Murray *personal communication* 2008
287 Ferguson Robert *personal communication* 2019
288 Winn Dick *personal communication* 2002

Gordon, Ida and Roy (back), Ellie, Janet holding baby Murray or Nora, William, Bertha (middle) and Janet, Dick and Betty (front)

without personal envy. He had extremely good manners – courtesy was an integral part of him.[289]

Both Dick and Murray thought that Bertha, who had come from a modest background, fully embraced the privileged life into which she married. She had staff – a cook, a housemaid, Nanny and a gardener called Mr Knee. She became good friends with members of the Eastern Suburbs' Establishment. Her best friend was Mabel Arnott of biscuit fame, continuing the close relationship between the two families that had started with the previous generation in Newcastle in the second half of the 19th century. Bertha was ever pressing Roy to participate in the traditional activities of men of his class and station, but Roy did not comply as much as Bertha would have liked.[290]

For Roy, intellectual stimulation was paramount. He pored over

---

289 Nield J *Speech to commemorate Roy Winn's death* 1974
290 Winn Murray *personal communication* 2008

analytical and scientific literature and read and analysed novels, plays and poetry. From Lawrence Durrell's *Alexandria Quartet* to the latest Patrick White novel, he sought and found new insights into human problems.[291] He continued his long interest in anthropology, ancient history and classics.

Despite his father's uncompromising temperance stand, Roy drank whisky in psychoanalytical seminars, claiming it assisted a weak ego to dissolve the most dangerous of all archaic structures, the superego.[292]

Dick always described Roy as a warm, tolerant, supportive and loving father but found his mother rather cold, never hugging or kissing him, even when he went off to war. Notwithstanding the emotional distance between mother and son, Dick loved her and found her ever ready to talk. There was plenty of happy and entertaining conversation at the family dinner table, from both parents, with Roy especially keen on an exchange of views. Dick said that he could talk to Roy about anything. High tea on Sunday night was especially memorable. It was Nanny's night off and the family would sometimes have pickled pork and salad. Controversial topics were regularly discussed and Roy would seek his children's thoughts and ideas. His sons felt secure enough to offer their own opinions on these and other weighty matters.[293]

Unlike most of the men of his generation, Roy was not a disciplinarian. Although Dick saw himself as a difficult and uncooperative child who caused a lot of worry to his parents and endlessly needled them, he was whacked only once, when Roy lost control over his usually very well controlled emotions. Murray also only remembers being hit once, when he opened the latch on the car door while it was in motion. Murray considered that Roy had good reason to be angry and speculated that Roy hit him out of fear.[294] Betty recalled that she had a small

---

291 Nield J *Speech to commemorate Roy Winn's death* 1974
292 Nield J *Speech to commemorate Roy Winn's death* 1974
293 Winn Murray *personal communication* 2008
294 Winn Murray *personal communication* 2008

Harold, Gordon, Dick, Roy c. 1939

accident in the family car while learning to drive. She was surprised how reasonable Roy was with her, in that he treated it as a good learning experience and showed no anger.[295]

Roy had tolerant, open-minded views about sexuality. It was a subject that was able to be discussed frankly at the dinner table. One evening he took Dick to the local church hall for a lecture at a meeting of the Young Men's Christian Association. Roy did not want to go but either felt it was his duty or was persuaded by Bertha. The lecture was on 'self abuse' but the lecturer talked about the subject in a very convoluted way and both Roy and Dick thought it a bit odd.[296]

On another occasion, Roy advised Dick that in order to make sure that the 'chosen girl' was really the 'right one', there were three important steps to undertake before making any marital commitment. The

---

295 Ferguson Robert *personal communication* 2019
296 Winn RW *Memoirs of Richard (Dick) Winn* 2003 p11

first was to get her drunk to see if she became aggressive; the second was to take her camping with no possibility of washing, to see if her real smell was sexually appealing; and the third was to have sex, to see if you were sexually compatible.[297] Although this must have been startlingly frank at the time, Dick thought it was such good advice that in the late 1960s he passed on the same words of wisdom to his own children.

Roy was not immune to the calls the Establishment made on men like him.

In November 1930, he joined the United Grand Lodge of NSW, through the Freemasons Lodge of Sydney University. Dick thought that, although Freemasonry was widespread among Protestants, it was curious his father had joined; it did not seem to fit his individualistic personality. Dick supposed that Bertha encouraged Roy to join as another mark of an Establishment figure.

Around the same time, the Royal Sydney Golf Club, which was fast losing members, went on a recruitment drive and invited Roy to join.

Horse riding mid-1930s: Murray, Roy, Betty

---

297 Winn Dick *personal communication* 2002

Images of Roy as a one-legged golfer teeing off at the first hole caused great mirth at home and Roy sensibly refused membership.

In 1939 Roy was on the school council of Cranbrook, where Dick and Murray went to high school. Dick believed it was Bertha who encouraged Roy to take such a position as he had little interest in Establishment roles. Iven Mackay was headmaster, strict but fair and well liked. A problem arose when his wife started to interfere in the running of the school, even going into the Masters Common Room, which was strictly by invitation only. Mackay seemed unable to curb her actions and the council reluctantly decided the headmaster had to go. This divided the school and the bitterness lasted for years. Dick believed that those years on the council were not easy for Roy.[298]

During the 1920s, the Winns had a weekender at 2 Fitzstubbs Avenue in Wentworth Falls, in the Blue Mountains west of Sydney, where the family went during the summer to escape the humidity of the city. The weekender was called Weeroona and was surrounded by trees,

Weeroona: Wentworth Falls holiday house

---

298 Winn RW *Memoirs of Richard (Dick) Winn* 2003 p19

on a hill on the west side of the rail line. Various branches of the family would meet there and take long walks in the bush. During long stays, the men of the family would walk to Wentworth Falls Railway Station and commute to work in the city. As well as Weeroona, Roy also took the family on camping holidays with the McMurtries to Lake Conjola on the state's South Coast and to a Cox's River farm where they rode horses.

Owing to his wooden leg, Roy was not able to participate in the usual range of sports like golf and tennis that men of his set played. Instead he took to the water, fishing and swimming. He hired what he called a 'pulling boat' from sheds at Double, Rose or Watsons Bays, and rowed himself around the harbour, a common Sunday occurrence. He said that he did it for exercise and fresh air.[299] He would also regularly swim one mile at Watsons Bay baths with his great friend Ken Felton, who was a master at Cranbrook.

He took the children on many outings and bought them treats of brandy snaps and ice-cream afterwards. He took Dick surfing at Bondi, and Dick and Betty to swim laps at Bondi Baths. Roy also bought Dick a clinker-built canoe[300] and a Vaucluse Junior (the Vee-Jay) sailing boat. Roy was reportedly good with his children's friends, such as Betty's life-long friend Binkie Bowker, as well as their cousin Janet, who remembered fondly that he visited her and brought her a book when she was in hospital. Janet said that Roy and her father Harold would make bows and arrows for all the children[301] and that Roy was a good conversationalist with children, being sincere and friendly, although this did not stop her being disturbed by his crutches.

Fishing remained a passion for Roy. During the Christmas school holidays, Roy would take Bertha and the children to the Hylands Hotel[302]

---

299 Winn RW *Memoirs of Richard (Dick) Winn* 2003 p9
300 Clinker is a method of boat building where the hull planks overlap each other
301 Winn Janet *personal communication* 2008
302 Now called O'Brien's Hotel

at Narooma on NSW's Far South Coast for a two-week vacation. This tradition continued for many years and was later taken up by Betty and Gordon and other members of the Ferguson family. When Roy and Bertha went to Hyland's, game fishing was one of the attractions but it appears that the only family members fishing were Roy and Dick. They often went out on Ben Badley's 32-foot commercial fishing boat.

In the summer of 1937–8, at the 150th anniversary of the local fishing competition, Roy was trawling a baitfish when he got a big strike and played it until the line went dead. When he reeled in, the head of a big hammerhead shark was attached but the body had been bitten clean off by something much larger.[303] Roy christened the thieving shark 'Monty'. It had a worn and jagged dorsal fin and was so big the skipper initially thought it was a whale.[304] Dick remembered seeing it swim under the boat and it appeared to him as though its width

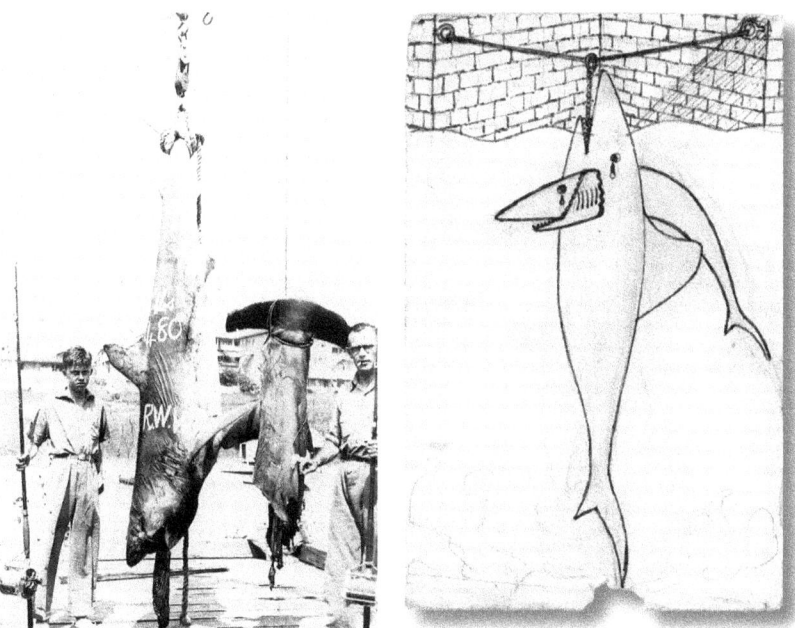

Left: Shark fishing, Narooma 1938: Dick and Roy   *Right*: Roy's drawing of Monty

303   Winn RW *Memoirs of Richard (Dick) Winn* 2003 p14
304   Winn Roger email communication 27 January 2019

was half its length, a truly enormous creature that could rival South Australian tuna fishermen's tales of their local great white shark monster. According to Roger,[305] Roy wrote an article about the incident for a fishing publication under the pseudonym 'medico'. The shark clearly made a great impression on Roy and he repeatedly drew and wrote 'of sharks and men… especially of Monty'. A Monty poem appeared in his booklet *Challenges to Mental Combat and Crackpottery* under the title *Cannibalism*[306] and Roy's novel *Men May Rise* also has an anecdote about shark fishing off Narooma.

Dick had many stories about fishing for shark and marlin off Narooma and Montague Island with his father. We have some 16mm film footage of seals swimming around a small boat in choppy seas, presumably taken in 1930s in the same area. Roy and Dick clearly shared a love of the ocean and the excitement of fishing for big game. However, there were limits to what they would hunt and both were very remorseful when they saw that someone had harpooned a dolphin to be used for bait. They vowed they would never use anything other than fish for that purpose.[307]

After going to Narooma for years, Bertha felt a change of holiday location was needed. Knowing how important fishing was to Roy, she arranged a trip to the Hotel Kosciuszko where trout fishing was on offer. I presume that again it was only Roy and Dick that fished, but at least the Hotel Kosciuszko was a smart place full of Bertha's sort of people. Murray remembers skiing holidays at Charlotte's Pass in the winter.

The family often travelled by car, a khaki-coloured Austin with the number plate 646666. Roy loved driving and tinkering with cars and serviced it at home. He would put soap under his fingernails to stop the grease from staining his fingers, a trick continued by Dick when he became an ophthalmic surgeon. Given that Roy's chain-smoking left him with brown-yellow nicotine stained fingers, the practice seems

---

305 Winn, Roger *personal communication* 2019
306 Winn RC *Challenges to Mental Combat and Crackpottery by Sujester* undated
307 Winn RW *Memoirs of Richard (Dick) Winn* 2003 p14

a bit pointless until one remembers how completely acceptable it was in those days for men to smoke whenever and wherever they wished.

Roy's lack of thrift and poor money management hit home in the early 1930s as the Great Depression deepened. By 1933, Roy and Bertha had moved to live in a rented property at 7 Gilliver Ave, Vaucluse, with the telephone number FU 8118. According to Dick, this change of address and circumstances was the result of some 'stupid' financial decisions on Roy's part,

Photo taken for Dick in POW camp c.1944: Roy, Murray

overlaid by the Depression. Dick said that Roy had no business sense but, at the urging of his father William, he had bought a large block of land opposite Quambaar School in Victoria Road, Bellevue Hill, with a view to building an architect-designed house.

When the Depression really started to bite, the bank asked him to repay the loan on the land, as well as his existing overdraft, and Roy was forced to sell the land at a loss. Needing money to buy consulting rooms in Macquarie Street, he sold the Bellevue Hill house to a fellow Freemason but always felt he had been 'taken down' by him and gradually gave up active membership.[308] Funds from his share in Winn's Ltd kept the family afloat but he had to let the cook and the housemaid go: leaving Nanny to take over all the housekeeping roles.

---

308 Winn RW *Memoirs of Richard (Dick) Winn* 2003 p10

In 1940, one year into the Second World War, Dick decided he wanted to join the Air Force. Bertha was not keen on the idea but Roy said it was Dick's decision alone. Dick already knew how to fly as he had had lessons as a boy and he thought Roy approved of his desire to enlist and was proud of him.[309] While Dick was flying fighter planes in North Africa, Bertha unexpectedly had a high blood pressure stroke and died on 20 June 1942 after a month of incapacity at home. She was only in her fifties. It took two months for the news to reach Dick who was finally told of his mother's death by Alan Ferguson, his commanding officer but also the brother of Betty's husband Gordon.

Bertha was buried in the large Winn plot at Rookwood Cemetery where William Winn and his mother Harriet were buried. Although Roy's untitled poem on the last page of this book suggests that he was deeply saddened by his beloved's death,[310] Murray said Roy was very stoical and found great solace from listening to classical music after dinner.

Roy's poor money management seems to be confirmed both by the 1921 letter about his financial extravagance noted earlier and by a 1945 letter in which he reveals that he is now out of debt as a result of some efforts at saving – assisted by being a widower.[311] Although not at all in his father William's

Bertha 1940

---

309 Winn RW *Memoirs of Richard (Dick) Winn* 2003 p21
310 Winn RC *I am a man* poem undated
311 Winn RC *Letter to Betty* 1945

league as a canny investor, Roy was interested in money in an intellectual way. He liked to discuss shares and various investments with Betty's husband, Gordon, who had a serious interest in the stock market. Roy had not had much success investing on his own and welcomed the hours spent talking about the market.[312]

On 10 January 1945, while Dick was in a prisoner-of-war camp in Germany, after his fighter plane had been shot down in North Africa, Roy married Nell Birkenhead Gale[313] at St Mark's, Darling Point. After the war, when Dick got to know Nell, he said she was a wonderful person and the best stepmother anyone could have.[314] Murray also spoke warmly of her.

Nell was the daughter of Walter Gale, a retired bank manager and noted amateur astronomer, and Violet Birkenhead of Waverley.[315] Nell was born in 1905 and married Roy when she was 39 and he was 54. She miscarried in the early years of their marriage and did not bear Roy any children. She had a Bachelor of Piano and had formerly been employed to play for passengers on cruise liners in the Pacific. She taught music at St Catherine's School, Waverley.

Nell owned 116A Bower Street, Manly, a magical two-storied weatherboard sea captain's cottage, known as 'The Castle'. It

Nell 1945

---

312 Ferguson Robert *personal communication* 2019
313 Nell Winn 1905–1995
314 Winn RW *Memoirs of Richard (Dick) Winn* 2003 p6
315 Walter Gale discovered three comets

had an absolute waterfrontage onto Fairy Bower and Shelley Beach and a wild garden of arum lilies, carnations and bananas in which she was a keen gardener. Roy invented a garden tool for her to remove onion weeds *in toto*, including all the satellite seeds that were usually left behind when the plants are pulled from the soil. It was a metal cylinder with pointed end to enter the soil and side access to remove the soil and seeds. He never put this into production but made several for friends who used them with great success.

Roy described the garden in his undated poem of the same name.

> With terraced walls of rough hewn mossy stone
> Sub-tropical garden steps to meet the sea
> A painted canvas thickly spread with vivid green
> And splashed with every note of colour
> The gay poinsettia's scarlet tinted leaves
> The frangipane's scented yellow blossoms
> And bougainvilleas decking wooden columns
> With floral strands of red or purple pennants
> Entwining there with blue convolvuli
> The entrance gate is flanked by soaring palms
> A Kentia tall and graceful Bangalan
> Gigantic fig tree spreads its curving arms
> In benediction over ground below.

Roy opening army disposal container

Roy moved to The Castle with Nell in 1946. His grandson Robert says its phone number was XU4456. The sitting room was full of dark barley-twisted Jacobean-style furniture, as well as Nell's Steinway piano on which she played her favourite Chopin pieces, especially in the evenings. She loved Debussy's *Claire de Lune*, which raised the hairs on the back of Robert's neck when it was played as the moon rose over the Pacific Ocean.[316]

Roy's poem *A Song* captures both his love of Nell and of music. It shows a very different man from the one who was asked about his virginity in Egypt.

> As cadence of the singer woos the heart
> A virginal angina joys the breast
> The singer and the hearer become one
> A mutual abandon unseen link
> The flowing tide of music fills them both
> With every ebbing wave the waters rise
> The climax to the passion urgent is
> A flooding through the lock gates of the heart
> A deepened satisfaction follows bliss
> A tender mood of quiet ensues
> An aftermath of pleasure is reward
> A rosy hue of gladness in the end.

I remember the Castle well. It was like a cubby house with nooks and crannies hosting the occasional treasure, like the splendid sperm whale's tooth that lived in Roy's small study under the stairs. To my eyes, it had a glamorously modern en-suite bathroom off the master bedroom and, in the main toilet, revolting old-fashioned shiny toilet paper with no absorbency. Affixed to the back of the toilet door was a promotional calendar from the local motor garage. Each month had its own page, with a jokey cartoon image and lined squares to write up appointments.

---

316 Ferguson Robert *personal communication* 2019

The Castle 1960: Nell with Matador, Roy, Helen, Evelyne, Dick, Vi Gale, and (front) Margaret, Philippa, Daniel, Roger

I didn't always get the jokes and I couldn't understand why the lined squares were always empty. The toilet had a distinctive, although not unpleasant smell – a curious brew of wood, paint, paper and salt spray.

My brother Roger and our cousins Robert and Cathy also have strong positive memories of the house but Roger didn't think it was as warm and welcoming as the Northbridge house in which our other grandparents lived. There was not much room to play and explore, and many rooms were out of bounds for children.[317]

The Castle was the first house that Cathy had been inside with stairs and she found it great fun to sleep upstairs in the middle room and hear the sounds of the ocean at night.[318] When Robert and Cathy were boarders at Cranbrook and Ascham, they regularly visited and found Nell easy to talk to and always very welcoming and friendly. Her

---

317 Winn Roger *personal communication* 2019
318 Jarratt Cathy *personal communication* 2019

The Castle 1961: Evelyne, Margaret, Daniel, Roger, Helen with baby Dominique, Roy, Philippa, Dick

afternoon teas were renowned for their homemade lemon cakes. On Sundays, when Nanny had her day off, there were cold meats, salads and gravy, and a lot of tasty left-over custard-based desserts. Cathy remembers Nell's Dachshund, Matador, farting under the table.[319]

Roy and Nell loved living near the sea. Nell walked to Shelley Beach for an early morning swim every day, telling Cathy that she always had a cold shower afterwards as it made her feel good, even on a cold day. Roy explored the rocky coastline between Fairy Bower and Manly, where he found wonderful seaweeds, fish and molluscs. He built himself a homemade glass and aluminium face-mask to better observe the sea life.[320] John Dakin, Professor of Zoology at Sydney University and author of *Australian Seashores*, was a great friend of his and the book a constant reference.

---

319 Jarratt Cathy *personal communication* 2019
320 Ferguson Robert *personal communication* 2019

Most mornings, Roy would walk the few steps to the shoreline rocks, unhitch his wooden leg, place it on the rocks and swim. I was very self-conscious about this public viewing of his withered stump and ungainly hopping about on one leg, and resisted accompanying him. I found the stench of stale cigarette smoke that was like a miasma around him off-putting and, like Robert, was very aware of the nicotine streak, not just on his fingers but running from his mouth to his nose and forehead, almost like a Hindu with symbolic markings on his forehead.

As well as the face mask and onion weed tool, Roy was good at making other things. He once built a skid board for Robert to skim along the shallow water left by the receding waves at low tide. Roy bought the marine ply timber and shaped, sanded and varnished it. Robert was quite taken aback by the gift, over which Roy had gone to so much trouble.[321]

Notwithstanding the tinkering and the swimming, most of Roy's time seems to have been spent researching, reading, thinking and writing. He would take Matador for walks, keenly observe the dog's smelling and toilet habits and would return home to write copious notes on quadrupeds and how they staked their territory, mated and hunted.[322] He would write poems and psychoanalyse plays – the psychoanalytical comments marked on the pages in fountain-pen ink. He would read journals. Hours were spent in his study at his vast desk, immersed in psychoanalytical books while chain-smoking. When Murray came second in his physics honours year at Sydney University, he went into his father's study to tell him the result and Roy, without looking up from his desk, said 'that's nice son' and returned to his reading.[323] Murray never forgot this incident but seemed more bemused than upset by it.

When I knew Roy, he found it difficult talking on the phone – he was deaf and wore two hearing aids connected to his wide black-rimmed

---

321 Ferguson Robert *personal communication* 2019
322 Ferguson Robert *personal communication* 2019
323 Winn Murray *personal communication* 2008

spectacles. I don't know when he started to lose his hearing but, given his novel's descriptions of the relentless shelling, I would be surprised if it hadn't begun on the Western Front. It is hard to know how much his inability to hear affected his communication with others and contributed to his retreat to the consolations of his study.

Uncle Murray's wife, Evelyne thought that deafness, along with inadequate French, were factors in Roy's lack of smiling engagement when they met for the first time at her wedding to Murray in Paris in 1954. The following year, when she returned to Australia with Murray and moved in with Roy and Nell at Manly for a short period, she thought it might be more to do with his personality than his hearing. She said that he made no attempt to get to know her or ask questions about her former life in France. And, even when she came second in her Bachelor of Arts at Sydney University, he did not congratulate her. She did not feel any animosity from him, just a barrier. She couldn't get anywhere with him.[324]

This is in keeping with Robert's description of Roy as quiet and studious and rather withdrawn, except at mealtimes when he was challenged by a thought or statement which raised his particular interest. By the time Evelyne and I encountered him, he was an old, deaf man with an ulcer, who had spent a professional lifetime listening intently to his patients and now favoured being left alone to pursue his own thoughts and unconventional interests.

Daniel's Christening 1958: Roy (back second right), Evelyne (front) with baby

---

324 Winn Evelyne *personal communication* 2008

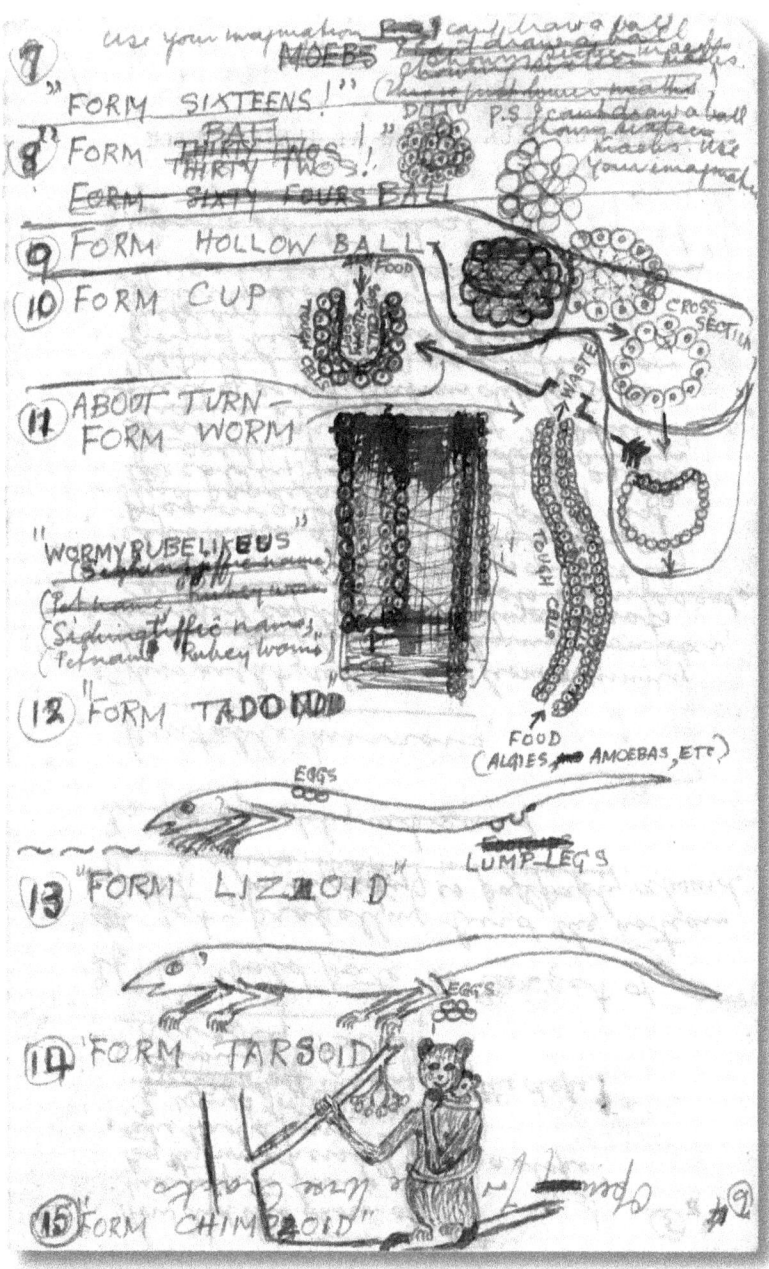

Chapter headings for Roy's Ideography

8

Poems and Nonsense Verse

Roy did not produce many psychoanalytical papers for publication, but over the course of his life he wrote prolifically. Although his novel *Men May Rise* appears to be a serious attempt to record and make sense of his own fraught experience of the war and its aftermath, much of his other extant writing is lighthearted, playful and very idiosyncratic.

There are scores of poems, riddles and proverbs written for his own and his children's entertainment and many of these are laced with musings on life and psychoanalytical matters.

The two major works in this latter category are *My Ideography* and *Challenges to Mental Combat and Crackpottery*. Both have been re-written numerous times with slight modifications. Roy confessed to his colleagues that he needed 'to write and rewrite before I get things clear'[325] and one suspects that this applied not only to psychoanalytical concepts but also to his poems.

My Ideography is a curious piece that seems to be trying to understand the development of the organs of the human body by comparison with lower order life forms. It interweaves Roy's interests in anatomy and physiology, anthropology, Freudian analysis and evolution. Its headings include *My Bearings*, *Human Embryo and Specialisation*, *Mind*, *Locomotion*, *Digestion*, *Bodily Matrix*, *Reproduction* and *Bisexuality*.

---

325 Winn RC *Psychotherapy* paper for Australian Association of Psychiatrists 7 November 1955

Roy said that *My Ideography* is his conception of human life presented in a schematic manner, in much the same way that the pictorial conventions of mural paintings inside the pyramids of Egypt reveal the objective life of its ancient peoples. I found a number of versions, some typed, some hand-written and many with corrections and additions. It was clearly a work to which he returned for re-working time and time again.

The single-celled life form, the amoeba, is a recurring motif in *My Ideography* and it graces all sorts of his other writings about the

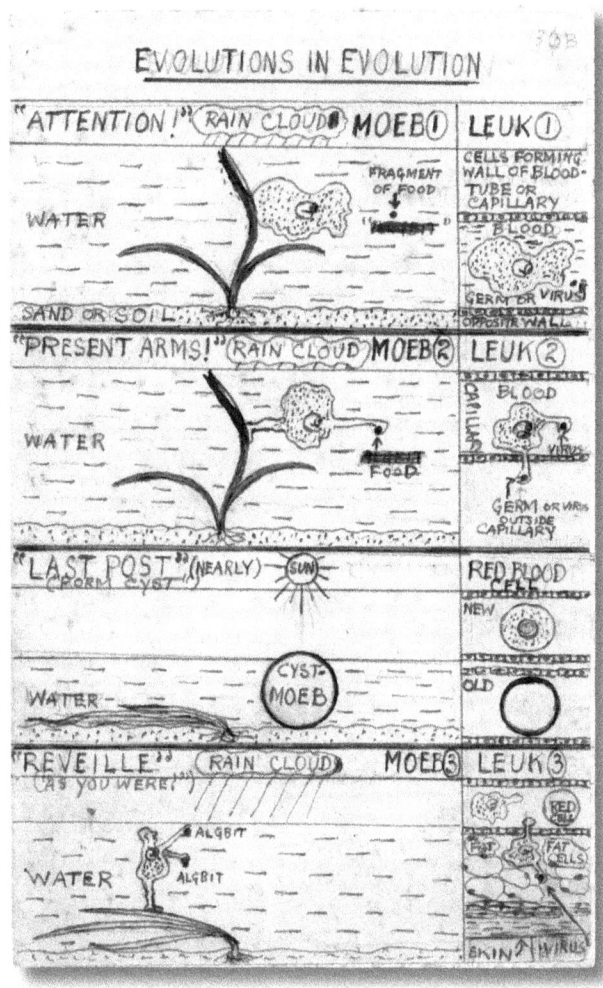

Evolutions

origins and progress of life. The authorship of different versions of *My Ideography* is invariably attributed to A. Mebb or sometimes A. Meeb.

For Roy, 'every man suffers from the delusion that he is an individual, whereas he is a state comprising millions of citizens. What is more, these citizens live together in a condition of uneasy truce, which at any moment may give place to civil war. In other words, just as peace is the interval between wars, so health is the armistice between the body and disease producing cells'.[326] Roy asks the reader to imagine human skin cells as encysted meebs and the body as a movable pond.

Roy wrote a number of other delightful poems about amoebae, some quite long. One I particularly like is called *Evolution*, which appears to be a simplified presentation of Roy's argument in *My Ideography*.

> For countless ages
> Had amoeba lived
> Unseen
> In wayside pool
> 'Till man, intent on stars
> Discovered glass
> Then tired of gazing heaven's silent face
> Looked down
> And saw himself reflected in the slime.
>
> Homunculus
> Approaching food; escaping danger
> Repopulating puny puddle world!
> Epitome of man
> Yet part of man
> Amoeba's image courses through man's veins
> And every tiny cell's amoeboid…[327]

---

326 Winn RC *My Ideography by A. Mebb* undated draft
327 Winn RC *Evolution* poem undated

Another poem, *Amoeba* follows a similar theme.

> A sea change, rich and strange
> Entropic no, homeostatic yes
> Immortal generation, living death
> Man's leucocyte, man's bone
> Man's mother, father, son
> Man's self.[328]

Roy's second major work was *Challenges to Mental Combat and Crackpottery*, authored, not by A. Meeb this time, but by Sujester. Its

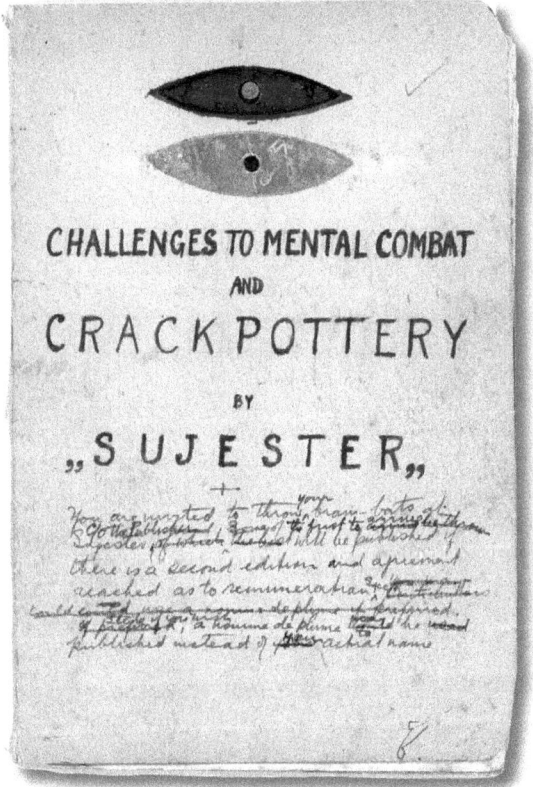

Challenges to Mental Combat booklet cover

---

328 Winn RC *Amoeba* in *My Ideagraphy by A. Mebb* undated

title page invites engagement with the work – the reader is asked 'to throw your brainbats at Sujester via the publishers. Some of them will be published. If there is a second edition and agreement reached as to remuneration: nom de plume being optional and prose preferred'.

Challenges to Mental Combat and Crackpottery is a collection of various writings: 30 poems called Crackpots; 10 verse-form riddles called Vriddles; four printer's-error riddles called Priddles; four modified proverbs called Mroverbs; along with introductions, suggestions, an interlude, an appendix and a last word. The titles of the poems include *Other Riddles of the Sphinx*, *Who's Who*, *Macquarie Cocktail*, *If You Like It*, *Owed to Ourcellves*, *This Bit of the Sky Belongs to Us* and *Sez You*.

As well as a certain preoccupation with amoebae and cells, *Challenges* includes many scientific and historical subjects: worms (*Lumbricus terrestris* and *Lumbricus agricola*); snails; sharks; pigeons; robots, the solar system, Newton and gravity, ancient Greek science and philosophy; Aristotle; Einstein and relativity; Scherezade (sic) and Arnold Toynbee.

Roy says that you can 'earn ten marks if you decipher the subject of any one of the Vriddles together with the significance of each concept

Illustration for Roy's Sherezade poem

in it, as understood by Sujester. You qualify for a reward of ten pounds (Australian) if you are the first to decipher the subject and all the concepts…'[329] *Challenges* is too long to include verbatim but for those who want a taste of its content and an inkling about their chances of winning the reward, I offer the following:

> The first Vriddle: 'If you glean a grain of truth within these sanguine pages, you are far from being vegetarian readers.'
>
> The fourth Priddle: 'What's a daddy mummy?'
>
> The Second Mroverb: 'Love makes the world go round and round.'
>
> The second Crackpot: 'If my bald pate is target of a jet propelling bird, the notion that I'm lucky is palpably absurd.'

If you are having difficulty deciphering the first Vriddle, you may get some inspiration from some notes I found to the third Vriddle called *Seven Carpets of Scherazade* which reads:

> 'A hopeful piscator untimely girds his loins.'
> Note: fisherman starting out.
>
> 'A whirlpool pattern swirls
> On eerie carpet in faint penumbral light.'
> Note: Whorls made by currents on the surface of the calm sea at dawn.
>
> 'A charioteer, a hunting, fires a bolt
> Shedding a primal tinge of blood;
> Further shafts on air releasing
> Exultantingly he scans the miniated field.'
> Note: The sun rises and reddens the sky.

---

329 Winn RC *Challenges to Mental Combat and Crackpottery* undated

'Immortal symbol mirrored briefly
Within the eyes of mortals
Is multiplied a thousand times.'
Note: The sun which mortals can only glance at, rises sufficiently high to be reflected in the sea.

'A mortal views aloft the glorious vestments
Worn by an ancient god.
An opal gem is set within a fiery ring.'
Note: The sun is seen at its zenith.

'A luckless piscator embroiders tales.'
Note: The fisherman exaggerates his experiences.

Not all Roy's riddles and proverbs found their way into the *Challenges* and I cannot resist including examples of his singular expression with its classical allusions.

Riddle One:
'In the halls of fame, she's a notorious name.
She was her brother's wife, her lover threatened strife.
She failed to lead the fight, and died from serpent's bite.'

Riddle Four:
'Helen must have had a busy time, cracking bubbly launching a thousand ships.
I am having difficulty with rhyme, writing after sinking a thousand sips.
How did Helen have the time to do, all the things that brought about the launchings?
Did she do much more than bill and coo, in the intervals between the jauntings?'

Roy's Mroverbs include:
» Everything comes to him who hates
» More waist less speed

- » Who incites and runs away, may have to fight another day
- » Two blacks wrong don't make whites right
- » The early bird lets sleeping dogs lie
- » Many beds aren't better than one
- » A man's work is now or never
- » Blood is thinner than mortar

Roy's archive holds at least five slightly different versions of the *Challenges* and he sent versions to his children for comment. He was agreeably surprised by their generous markings, and gratified that he could accept adverse opinions.[330] He wrote a poem to them in response:

> Now I have due time to bide
> If I were a poet I'd
> Thank you both in glorious verse
> For your high critique so terse
> With such subtle perspication
> And enlightened estimation.

Illustration for Roy's sphinx poem

---

330 Winn RC *Letter to Sun and Arb* undated

In 1960, Roy wrote to the editor of *The Sydney Morning Herald* offering two items of comic verse that commented on articles that appeared in its March newspapers. He mentioned that he was intending offering to book publishers Angus and Robertson a collection of his nonsense verse for publication, in order to help fund his currently unpaid medical research.[331]

This episode gave me pause. Revealing that he intended to write to Angus and Robertson in order to fund his research seems naïve, and imagining that the content and presentation of his curious verse would be of any interest to such a publisher makes me wonder at his lack of worldliness. Roy's novel, with its wooden dialogue and simplistic emotional responses, hints at his initial difficulty in appreciating the emotions of others. His combative psychoanalytical papers suggest a lack of understanding about the most effective way of arguing against entrenched views.

---

331 Winn RC *Letter to SMH* 28 March 1960

THE CONTINUAL INNER SEARCH

Roy 1943

9

Last Words

In early 1963 Roy developed ulceration of his amputation stump, which necessitated the use of crutches instead of his wooden leg. Soon after, he fell and injured his left knee. That led to poor sleep and anxiety about whether he would walk again. Jaundice followed and he was admitted to Concord Veterans' Repatriation Hospital. He was to have an X-ray and was told not to eat anything. Dick said Roy forgot and ate a banana, which upset the resident medical officer, who was not able to successfully perform the X-ray and make a diagnosis.

Dick always thought that Roy deliberately 'forgot' as he did not want to prolong his dying – Roy was not afraid of death. When Roy developed severe abdominal pain, Dick said that the staff did not believe him and the family found it too distressing to stay in the room and see Roy's extreme pain at the end. He died on 17 August 1963 at the Concord Hospital holding Dick's hand.[332] The cause of death was a perforated chronic prepyloric ulcer and peritonitis.

Roy was cremated at the Northern Suburbs Crematorium. Dick and Murray scattered his ashes from a rowing boat off Fairy Bower where he had regularly swum.

Roy did not believe in resurrection[333] but he wrote a beautiful, undated poem that gives hints about his views on immortality:

---

332 Winn RW *Memoirs of Richard (Dick) Winn* 2003 p7
333 Winn RW *personal communication*

> Each man's a drop upon the sea of time
> Evaporates and leaves invisive[334] trace
> Returns again its absence to efface
> Perchance from cloudbank in some far-off clime
> No man has ever writ eternal rhyme
> No man has sculpt a figure n'er endured
> No man forgetless memory secured
> Symphonic music by or stony line
> In the human book of knowledge it is said
> The gametes surely seek each other 'fore
> The cells that form our bodies are all dead
> The nearest to eternal now he said
> Most satisfying hope of human race
> Immortal history in a baby's face.

He left a simple will: all his Winn's Ltd shares to his children, the rest of his estate to Nell. It was a sad time for Nell, as in the same decade all her three sisters and two brothers died. Like the very practical person she was, she threw herself into the Manly Musical Society, delivering Meals on Wheels and playing bridge.[335] Nell died in March 1995. A wake was held at the Fairy Bower house. The Winn clan assembled to farewell her and the wonderful house. I seem to remember eating cake.

Although it had been a gamble to be the first full-time, privately practising psychoanalyst in Australia, Roy had pulled it off. With a little help from Winn's Ltd money, he was able to make a living as a psychoanalyst until his retirement. He was also able to nurture and expand psychoanalysis in Australia, connect it with the international field overseas and provide it with a well-functioning Sydney base for furthering the cause.[336] More

---

334 I think 'invisive' here means 'barely visible'
335 Winn Murray *Obituary of Nell Winn* 1995
336 In 1957 Roy asked his children to give his psychoanalytical books, including four volumes of Freud's collected papers, to the Sydney Institute of Psychoanalysts, after his death.

The Castle with view of Fairy Bower, Nell's wake 1995: Murray, Evelyne, Margaret, Dick, Helen, Andrew, Cathy, Ross Jarratt, Chris Meehan

importantly from Roy's point of view, he was able to help people understand themselves better through talking and looking deeply into the self. He left a legacy and it was acknowledged by his professional colleagues.

Frank Graham, a medical doctor who undertook psychoanalysis with Roy in 1939 before becoming a psychoanalyst himself, wrote an obituary and a memoire of Roy. He said that Roy 'was a sincere, committed psychoanalyst, always willing to listen to and to discuss usefully whatever came up'.[337] The *Medical Journal of Australia* said, 'few had such an acute insight into the unconscious mental processes. This insight, together with a considerable capacity for controlled speculation, made him a ready recipient of new ideas in psychoanalysis; and yet no one was quicker to distinguish the genuine constructive new idea from its imitation.'[338]

Roy's good friend and fellow analyst Janet Nield said he was

---

337 Graham FW 'Memoire of Roy Winn' *The Adelaide Review of Psychoanalysis* Vol. 7, No 3, November 1987
338 'Obituary of Roy Coupland Winn' *MJA* 29 February 1964 p334

'dedicated to the continual inner search to understand himself and others'.[339] Reg Martin, a fellow analyst, concurred, saying that towards 'his colleagues he was open and frank even about his own limitations and personality… he was at all times encouraging of those who were not yet qualified as analysts and at all times treated our work as though we were already analysts'.[340] According to Janet Nield, he never demanded omnipotence and did not believe he had the right to advise or admonish the young. He could be angry and attacking, yet he was humble and dignified. He was wise yet he was extremely youthful and joyous in his pleasure in life.[341]

He eschewed publicity and public controversy and always felt that work and more work, research and more research, would give the answers, not polemics.[342] He focused on his clinical work and was viewed as essentially a clinical practitioner, at his best in small discussion groups. According to Frank Graham, he 'had an impeccable classical technique in analysis… his intuitive insight was remarkable…'[343]

Frank also believed that there was general value in Roy's ideas – 'he found a lot to be seriously considered in the work of Melanie Klein and did some original thinking as regards the infant's crawling stage, leading to the biped stance and accompanying feelings of loss.'[344] Regrettably, Roy did not comprehensively develop his own line of research to offer evidence for his ideas. That was left to others. Frank Graham considered that Roy's work might well be the subject of further research.[345]

As a pioneer psychoanalyst in Australia, Roy had no one easily accessible to confer with, or to train him as a training analyst. This was a source

---

339 Nield J *Speech to commemorate Roy Winn's death* 1974
340 Martin R *Speech for the Inauguration of the Winn Library* 1993
341 Nield J *Speech on Roy Winn* Sydney analysts' meeting 1974
342 Graham F 'Obituary of Roy Winn' *MJA* February 1964 p333
343 Graham FW 'Memoire of Roy Winn' *The Adelaide Review of Psychoanalysis* Vol. 7 No 3 November 1987
344 Graham FW 'Memoire of Roy Winn' *The Adelaide Review of Psychoanalysis* Vol. 7 No 3 November 1987
345 Graham FW 'Memoire of Roy Winn' *The Adelaide Review of Psychoanalysis* Vol. 7 No 3 November 1987

of regret for Roy, and for Frank Graham, who believed that 'if anybody should have been a training analyst it was Roy Coupland Winn'.[346]

Even if Roy's clinical work was not classic psychoanalysis in Freud's terms, it nevertheless 'forged the foundation for much of what was to come'.[347] 'When no one in Australia cared about Freud, Roy communicated with him. When Ernest Jones of IPA was unknown, Roy was known to Ernest Jones'... he was 'the vital gallant force of our Australian analytic beginnings.'[348]

The early expectations of William Winn's boys were that they would lead lives of comfort, status and privilege, in return for upright and honorable service, under the umbrella of a robust conservative Methodism.

In many ways, these expectations were fulfilled in Roy, although their form changed in ways he could not have imagined in his youth. Notwithstanding the loss of the home they owned at Bellevue Hill, Roy and Bertha led a life of material comfort and, like the rest of the Winn clan, Roy maintained his Winn-related status and privilege throughout his years. Despite the scorn of many in the medical profession, Roy had both status and privilege within his small psychoanalytical world. He remained an upright and honourable man and, even though he dispensed with a personal belief in religion, he spent a lifetime serving the mental welfare of others. The boy missionary who wanted to save souls turned into a man intent on saving minds.

Evelyne's reflection on her early relationship with Roy and Murray's account of his father's response to his academic success, both accord with my own childhood experience of Roy: that he was a man so absorbed in his own world and so deeply focused on his own interests that he was somewhat disengaged from others. I now see a broader picture: an individualistic man, who spent his life on the inner search.

---

346 Graham FW 'Memoire of Roy Winn' *The Adelaide Review of Psychoanalysis* Vol. 7 No 3 November 1987
347 Ellingsen P *A History of Psychoanalysis in Australia* 2013 p85
348 Nield J *Speech to commemorate Roy's death* 1974

He was direct and somewhat naïve, marching to his own particular drum, rejecting unthinking conformity to social norms and doggedly pursuing individual, unpopular and unorthodox ideas, all for what he believed to be the greater good.

When I look at Roy's descendants, I see that some of these traits have spanned the generations. When my loving but atypical father, Dick, was writing his own memoir, he was so absorbed in his own world that he failed to include his beloved wife and children in the first draft, not because they didn't matter but simply because they failed to register on his radar at the time.

My side of the family is salted with non-standard models and peppered with Autism Spectrum diagnoses. Some of us are somewhat unworldly; some of us are very concrete in our thinking and oriented towards the factual and technical; some of us have difficulty articulating emotions; some of us demonstrate deep dependence on our beloveds, while struggling to really connect to other people; some of us view the world a bit differently from the norm; some of us are non-conformists and could be described as quirky or idiosyncratic. Perhaps Roy was the origin of this wonderful, rich, unconventional genetic thread? I expect he would have thought so:

> The cells that form our bodies are all dead
> The nearest to eternal now he said
> Most satisfying hope of human race
> Immortal history in a baby's face.

Each of us who knew Roy has our own particular impression of him, dependent on time, place and exposure. Yet, despite immersing myself in this biography, I do not think I know him well enough to provide a final analysis or summation. Perhaps his poetry gives a clue. His lifelong quest to 'understand' might well be captured in his poem *I am a Man*, where a lifetime of profound experiences can be encapsulated in simple single-celled existence. So, who better then to have the last word than Roy?

I am a man
Ecstasy I've felt and consternation
Wonder and dread
I've seen the sea reflect the light from distant planets
A pearly cloud presage the storm

I've heard the singing of my children
I've trembled at the roar of war
Exquisite the odour of my first-born
I've shuddered at the stench of death

I've touched responsive skin of my beloved
I've kissed her cold dead brow
I've read immortal yearnings of my forebears
And obituaries in rocks

I've followed stars on distant pathways
I've scanned my body cells
Leucocytes I learn amoeba are
And skin, a waterbag of cysted moebs
Encysted 'moebae too the lime encrusted bone
And fragile red cells
Our minds dependent are
On stretched amoebae
Linking skin and muscles
These being 'moeba's retracting pseudopodia.[349]

---

349 Temporary protrusion of the surface of an amoeboid cell for movement and feeding.

Appendix 1
Winn Family Tree

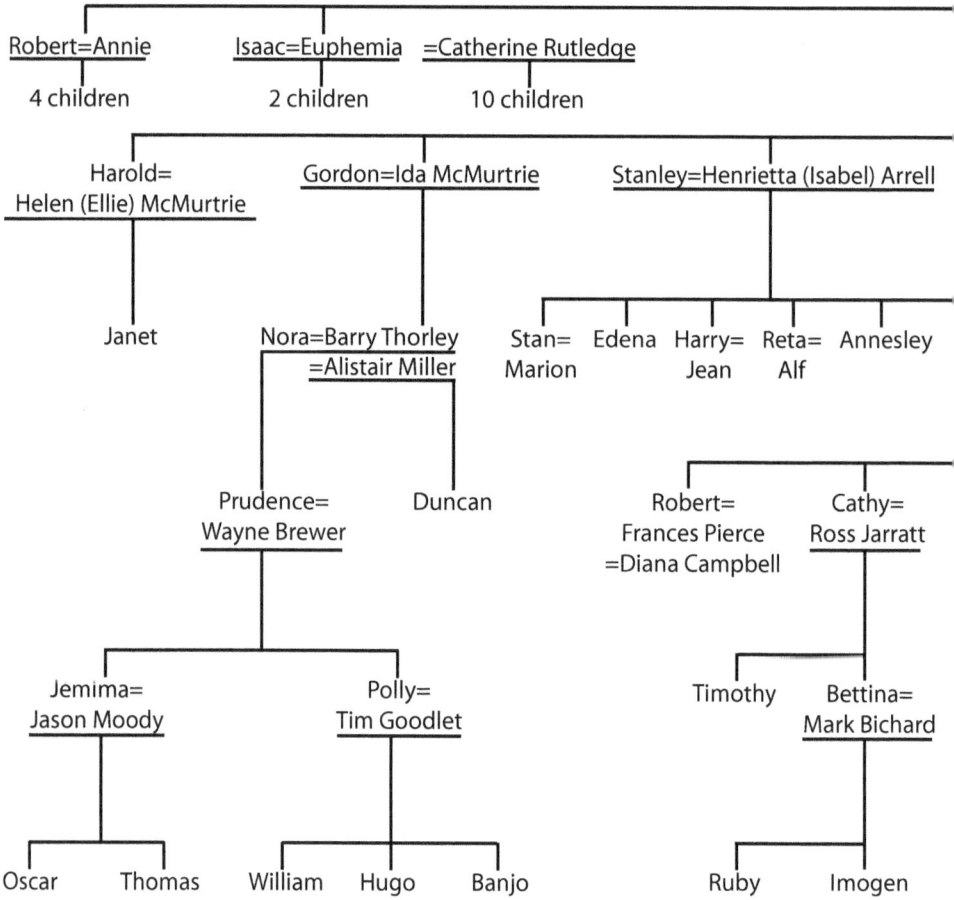

Winn Family Tree

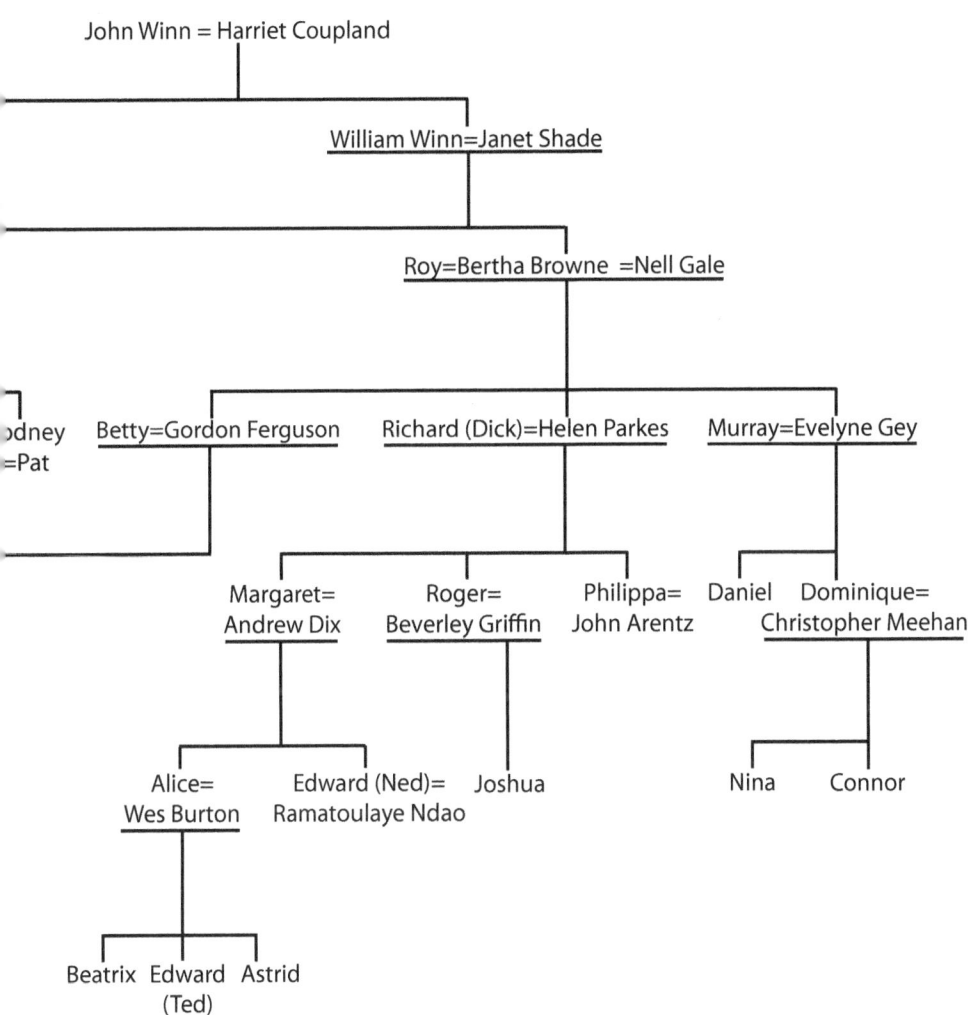

Winn's Newcastle stores, *from top left to right*: 1890s, 1900, 1911, 1920, 1924, 1950s

Appendix 2

William Winn and a Short History of Winn's Limited

Note: There is some repetition of text between this appendix and the biography itself. I wanted there to be a 'stand alone' appendix that family members could use for their own investigations into Winn history, obviating the need to repeatedly look for information widely scattered throughout the main body of the biography.

Early Winns

The Winn family was originally from Gwydir in North Wales, but in time some of its descendants became textile merchants in London. George Wynne of Gwydir was appointed draper to Queen Elizabeth I and his grandson Sir George Winn was created the First Baronet of Nostell in 1660. Nostell had previously been an Augustinian priory in West Yorkshire but was surrendered to Henry VIII in 1540 as part of the dissolution of the monasteries. Nostell passed through a number of owners until 1654, when it was purchased by Sir Rowland Winn. Three generations of Winns used the priory buildings, which they converted into a manor house.

The present house, which is still called Nostell Priory, dates to 1773 and is the work of the 4th and 5th Baronets, also called Sir Rowland Winn. It is a Palladian building with Robert Adam interiors, Chippendale furniture and a John Harrison clock, all set in 120 hectares of parkland. The family owed its subsequent wealth to coal under the estate and later from leasing land in Lincolnshire for mining iron ore for the Industrial Revolution. The Palladian house continued to be occupied by Winns until given to the National Trust in lieu of death duties in 1984. Betty Ferguson *née* Winn believed that our Winn family was descended from the Nostell Priory Winns, but I have not made any attempt to confirm this.

William Winn and his forebears

William Winn[350] was born to Harriet Coupland[351] and John Winn[352] also known as Isaac or James Winn. Harriet was one of 12 children of Joseph Coupland and Mary Johnson of Trusthorpe Lincolnshire. John and Harriet Winn married at Tealby, Lincolnshire, in 1844, and that same year arrived in Australia on the *Templar* as assisted migrants to the Australian Agricultural Company. They made their way to Newcastle and lived on Campbells Hill, Pitt Town.[353]

As well as William, Harriet and John had three other children: Robert,[354] who worked as a builder and married Annie Webb; Isaac,[355] who married Euphemia (Effie) Arnott in 1880 and then Catherine Rutledge in 1886; and Maria, who married John Kittson but died in childbirth in 1876 at King Street, Newcastle, leaving two boys aged five and six years old.

John was initially engaged as a carpenter for six months at 3 shillings and 6 pence a day. He died in 1855 at the Factory Lunatic Asylum, presumably from the head injury he suffered after falling drunk from a horse.

Harriet was a woman with 'great get up and go' and she passed this trait to William.[356] In 1856, she established a small shop in her Hamilton home (the first Winn store), which was on the site of the present St Peter's Church of England, Hamilton. The first Methodist

---

350 William Winn 1849–1929
351 Harriet Winn, née Coupland, later Clarke 1823–1908
352 John Winn 1815–1855
353 Pitt Town is now known as Hamilton
354 Robert Winn 1845-c1920
355 Isaac Winn 1852–1934
356 Winn Murray *personal communication* 2008

services in the area were conducted in her home in 1858.

Harriet produced and sold a medication called Coupland's Eradica, a preparation prescribed by orthodox doctors which eventually went out of fashion when antiseptics were introduced. It softened the skin and allowed foreign bodies and pus to escape from the tissues below the surface.[357] It was considered so effective it 'could draw a cork out of a bottle, blood from a stone and sixpence from the grasp of a Scot'.[358] Harriet's grandson, Roy Winn, a medical practitioner, continued to use it for splinters, pimples and boils. After John's death, Harriet remarried and was henceforth known as Harriet Clarke. Roy was present at her death, which was of long duration. 'She loved life and was so energetic that dying seemed to be the last thing she would consider.'[359] Harriet is buried in the Methodist section of Rookwood Cemetery, Sydney, next to her son William Winn.

Harriet Winn

Janet Winn née Shade and her forebears

Janet Winn[360] who was usually called Jessie, was five years older than William. She was the daughter of Thomas Shade, a painter, and Sophia Cameron, the second daughter of the 10 children born to Donald Cameron[361] and his first wife Anne McPherson. Thomas and Sophia married at St Andrew's Church, Sydney, in 1840.

---

357 Winn RC *Letter to Betty* 20 February 1961
358 Winn RC *Letter to Betty*, undated
359 Winn RC *Letter to Betty* 20 February 1961
360 Janet Winn 1845–1938
361 Donald Cameron 1777–1867

Sophia had come with her father to Australia as an assisted migrant on the *Brilliant* from Ardnamurchan, Argyllshire in Scotland in 1838. Donald's obituary notice said he was known as 'King of the Highlanders'. He was of Waterhole Reach Farm, now called Allworth Park, and had 15 children and 66 grandchildren, many of whom settled in the Hunter and Port Stephens area. He is buried at Stroud.

At the time of Janet's wedding in 1876, William was living at Camerons Hill, Hamilton but he married Janet at her parents' house at 5 Argyle Terrace, Pitt Street, Redfern.

William and Janet's children

William and Janet had four sons. The first was William Harold, born in 1883 and always known as Harold. He was eventually the director of Winn's Ltd in Newcastle. In February 1917 he married Helen (Ellie) McMurtrie[362] from Braeside at Lady Martins Beach, Wolseley Road, Point Piper and they had a daughter Janet Winn, a widely respected dietitian.[363] Harold died aged 64 in 1948.

The second son was Gordon Russell, born in 1887. He married Ida McMurtrie (Ellie's sister) in November 1916, and became managing director of Winn's Ltd Sydney. Gordon and Ida had a daughter Nora and a baby boy who died young. Their granddaughter is Pru Brewer.

The third son was Stanley Dickson, born deaf in 1889. It is likely that Stanley was schooled at the NSW Institution for the Deaf, Dumb and Blind, which was established in 1872 and was the first school and boarding facility for the deaf in Australia. Family lore is that William supported the institution financially. Stanley could 'deaf sign' but lip-reading was the main method of communication within the family. Stanley married Isabel Arrell who was not deaf when they met

---

362 The McMurtrie brothers (John, George and Archibald) established a very successful boot and shoe making business in 1864 and by 1900 its factory on the corner of Wells and Abercrombie Streets, Eveleigh employed over 300 staff and produced 7500 pairs of boots a week. The building still exists next to Redfern Station and is known as the Water Tower.

363 Harold's daughter Janet Winn should not be confused with her grandmother Janet (Jessie) Winn

but became so after an illness later in life. Stanley and Isabel had six children – Stanley, Harry, Edena, Reta, Annesley who was also deaf, and Rodney. Over time, Stanley's family participated less often at large family gatherings, most probably because of the communication difficulties encountered with large groups of people.[364] Stanley died aged 59, after being hit by a car.

The fourth son was Roy Coupland, born in 1890. Roy married Bertha Browne of Loddon in the United Kingdom. Roy and Bertha had three children: Betty[365] who married Gordon Ferguson; Richard (known as Dick)[366] who married Helen Parkes; and Murray[367] who married Evelyne Gey.

William and Janet had two other children who died at birth – a daughter, Jessie Harriet, in 1879, and a son in 1881.

Winn houses

When William married Janet Shade in 1876, the marriage certificate described him as a warehouseman from 1 Lydia Houses, Drummond Street, Carlton, Melbourne, so that is likely to be the time he was apprenticed there. By 1879 William and his brother Isaac had established a drapery business in Hunter Street Newcastle and their mother Harriet moved from Hamilton to be closer to them.

William's brother Robert was a builder and, sometime around the late 1870s to early 1880s, he built four terraces, numbers 34–40, on the western side of Perkin Street, Newcastle. Robert, William, Isaac and their families occupied the Perkin St terraces, presumably in order to be near the new Winn & Co premises. Janet's widowed sister Mary Ann (Marian) Aird also lived there. She was a co-founder of Winn & Co with William and Isaac. Her son John Cameron Aird also worked at the Winn shop. The terraces are still there and appear to be well maintained.

---

364 Winn Janet *personal communication* 2008
365 Betty Ferguson, née Winn 1919–2002
366 Richard Winn 1921–2007
367 Murray Winn 1927–2015

In 1878, the Winns built a Victorian house on two acres (0.81 hectares) of land at 15 Kerr Street, Mayfield. It had five bedrooms, bay windows, lacework verandahs, French doors, and extensive grounds with a coach house and stables, and was ostentatiously called Winnonaville. The grandeur of the house is attested by its 2019 sale, which set the record for highest purchase price of a non-development site in Mayfield.[368]

Sometime after 1889, the Winns bought an even larger residence on five acres (2 hectares) of land at 17 Section Street, Mayfield,

Winnonaville, 2019

---

368 Real estate sale notice, 2019

overlooking the Hunter River. It had been owned by the Arnotts who had established a successfully bakery business in Newcastle and was called Arnott Holme. The Winns and the Arnotts were great friends. After the purchase, the Winns changed its name to Winn Court and as late as 1919 Roy's brother, Harold Winn, was living there. The house is now called Annesley House and is part of a nursing home complex but it is in poor repair and much altered from the original.

The Arnotts reportedly purchased a Victorian house for their daughter Euphemia (Effie) when she married Isaac Winn. We understood the house to be Winnahra, a two-storey house at 21 Highfield St, similar in scale and style to Winnonaville. Winnahra stands on the same long Mayfield Ridge overlooking the Hunter River as Winn Court and is in remarkably good condition. Winnahra is dated 1890, but Effie died young in 1884, so it is unlikely to be the Arnott-purchased house. The other possibility is a single-storey house at 143 Crebert St, Mayfield, also reportedly built by the Arnotts as a wedding gift for their daughter,

Winnahra, 2019

Mayfield Ridge c.1890s with Winn Court far left and Winnahra far right
Scholey-Upfold Papers, University of Newcastle

but it is dated c.1896, which is also too late for Effie. The Arnott gift may well be apocryphal.

After William's stint in Melbourne, he moved between Sydney and Newcastle. In the early 1890s, he bought himself a mansion at Concord, possibly in Davidson Avenue, with a four-acre (1.6 hectares) orchard set in 20 acres (8.1 hectares) of pasture.

Later, when he became a well-established member of the business community of Sydney, he had a large, elegant residence called Rockley in Campbell St, Milsons Point.[369] It had extensive views across Sydney Harbour to Garden Island, Circular Quay and the Rocks, and the ferry that eventually brought cars between the south and north shores of the harbour. A full-time cook and housekeeper ran the house, providing a family lunch of 'roast chicken and hot plum pudding and cream every Saturday.'[370]

The lounge room was full of marvels brought back from various Winn trips overseas. There were black, carved dragon tables and huge Chinese vases, like something out of *Ali Baba and the Forty Thieves*. There were prizes from William's target shooting successes, including a fancy clock on the mantlepiece.[371]

---

369 I believe *Rockley* now has its entrance on the south side of Upper Pitt Street between Peel and Parkes Streets
370 Ferguson Betty *Recollections of Sydney Harbour before the Bridge* undated
371 Winn RW *Memoirs of Richard (Dick) Winn* 2003 p13

The Winns also owned an elegant holiday house called Weeroona at 2 Fitzstubbs Ave, Wentworth Falls. Ownership was in the name of Gordon's wife Ida from 1923–7. William's children and their families regularly took holidays there and used the train station to get to and from Sydney.

The only early Winn house I knew was that of William's son, Harold, who eventually ran the Newcastle Winn's Ltd. He built a lovely large turn of the century brick house on Fig Tree Point at Toronto. Single storey, it had wide verandahs and extensive grounds that included a tennis court, orchard and boathouse, all overlooking Lake Macquarie. When I knew it, before their daughter Janet died, it appeared to be in a time warp, with objects from Harold's heyday apparently still in their original position a half-century after his death. There was a phonograph and accompanying pile of 78 rpm records, works by Arthur Streeton and Sydney Long, and chinoiserie from William's buying trips to Asia. The wardrobes were filled with parental clothes. Once, we came across a 1916 newspaper – in a pile of magazines on a coffee table.

William Winn and Winn's Ltd

William, Isaac and Marian Aird had founded the drapery business, W Winn & Co, in Hunter Street, Newcastle in 1878. The brothers had gained some experience of business when they had assisted their mother in her small shop, and later when they took apprenticeships in a prominent wholesale drapery business in Melbourne.

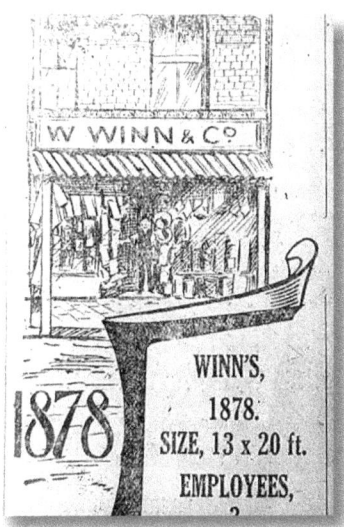

Winn's advertisement, 1878

Overseas trips and expansion to Sydney

In 1886, the brothers 'travelled to the home markets in London and Bradford, where with clever purchasing and good contacts made, the

Niagara Falls trip 1886: William Winn (back row, left), Anne Rutledge, Isaac Winn. Janet (front) holding baby Harold, Harriet Winn

store flourished'. William took his wife Janet and their young son Harold and, with Isaac and his new wife Anne, were away for over five months. They mixed business with pleasure, purchasing large quantities of goods for the firm from factories in Manchester, Glasgow and Belfast and seeing the sights including Niagara Falls, Venice, Naples, Lucerne, Milan, Florence and Rome. They stayed in accommodation on Russell Square in London and Janet, who was pregnant with Gordon during the trip, had him christened Gordon Russell on her return to Newcastle, in memory of their stay.[372]

The success of the trip encouraged William, and in 1893 he commenced new businesses in Sydney: at North Sydney, Balmain and Leichhardt. During these early years, William, who had tremendous energy, was always starting and changing businesses.[373] After some years he sold Leichhardt and in 1900 went back to Newcastle

---

372 Winn Janet *personal communication* 2008
373 Winn RC *Letter to Betty* 1961

to support Isaac who was presiding over a business in the doldrums. Once he had repaired things there, William arranged for Isaac's oldest son, also called William, to take over the running of Newcastle.

In 1903, the business became a limited liability company, with William senior and Isaac as governing directors. The firm's motto was 'the utmost quality with the best service' or, sometimes, 'the utmost in value at the lowest price'.

In 1906 William senior returned to Sydney for good and started new Winn's Ltd drapery businesses in Oxford Street, and in Botany Road, Redfern, and Camperdown, all of which proved successful. Things must have gone very well as, in about 1909, William was able to take his family on an extensive overseas tour including to Japan.

Expansion in Newcastle

In 1910 the original Newcastle shop was replaced by a three-storey building with fashionable and renowned luncheon rooms on the second floor overlooking Newcastle harbour. Further premises were acquired in 1912 in Newcastle. Business continued to go well and, in April 1920, Winn's Ltd hosted a welcome home picnic for 'returned boys (employees)'. A special train was hired and took picnickers from Newcastle to Toronto.

By 1922, Winn's Ltd stocked furniture, clothing, floor coverings and sporting goods and had an efficient mail-order business. Winn's Ltd marketed its own sewing machine, the Winnetta, and provided home deliveries free of charge.

> 'People soon found that a reliable article could always be found at Winn & Co, at a moderate price. Everything that an extensive and modern drapery and clothing emporium should contain was to be found at their store and the result was that the establishment was always more or less – invariably more – crowded. In fact, a day's shopping and a visit to Winn's were practically synonymous terms…'

> 'The business… [was] built on genuineness in advertising and honesty in selling.'

That may well be true, but William was also a canny businessman. His grandson, Dick Winn, tells the story of a sale of fire-and-water damaged bed linen. When all the discounted stock was sold but customers were still clamouring for more, William rushed to find undamaged stock in the storeroom, pulled the sheets to the floor, jumped on them with his street shoes and returned with them to the discount pile. Although he sold them at a reduced price, he still made a profit. He used to buy stock with a loan from the bank at 5 per cent and sell it at 7 to 10 per cent profit.[374]

In 1924 a fine new Winn's Ltd building was erected in Newcastle with an extra lift and such modern facilities as a sprinkler system. In 1928 Winn's Ltd had 628 employees and by 1929 it was known as 'one of the largest drapery businesses in the state'.

Winn's Ltd staff, philanthropy and good works

Winn's Ltd was noted for treating its staff well. William and Isaac were both 'staunch advocates of the early closing movement and shut their store at 6.30pm, greatly to the benefit and health of their assistants'.[375]

During the Great Depression, in an effort to be fair, all employees were interviewed about their home situation. Those in greatest need were given the most work. Those who were better off were stood down for several days weekly, while sole wage earners were given longer hours. Any food that was left over from the tearoom was always sent to the mission to be distributed to people in need.

There is a lovely account by Anne Griffiths of her 40 years working for Winn's Ltd, starting from 1921 as a 14-year-old. She viewed Winn's as 'one big happy family'.[376] Many staff worked at Winn's for decades and those that completed 25 years of service were given a gold watch, suitably inscribed. By 1928 there had been 16 recipients of these watches.

---

374 Winn RW *Memoirs of Richard (Dick) Winn* 2003 p13
375 Robertson, G *History of Winn's Ltd from October 1878 to 19 January 1980*
376 Robertson, G *History of Winn's Ltd from October 1878 to 19 January 1980*

Street parade and crowds outside Winn's Newcastle c. 1920s

The year 1928 was Winn's Ltd's 50th Jubilee at Newcastle and a big dinner was held for staff and family. Over the years there were not infrequent dinners for shareholders and staff to celebrate trading milestones and Winn's Ltd regularly produced elaborate floats for Newcastle's street parades.

Winn's Ltd management and staff were known for their generous donations to charity, including presenting the first motorised ambulance to Newcastle's ambulance superintendent. In 1941 Winn's Ltd staff members put on a musical review, *Just for Fun*, raising money for the Australian Imperial Force Ambulance Fund.

William promoted individual saving on the part of both employees and family members, through something called the Winn's Thrift Club. Personal accounts were set up, money was paid in and interest was earned. All William's grandchildren had accounts and, although Dick could not remember exactly how the scheme worked, by the time he was an adolescent he had accrued over £120 ($9,750 in current Australian dollar) – a very large sum for a boy in the early 1930s.

The end of Winn's Pty Ltd

In 1948, Winn's Ltd became a public company. It remained a moderately successful business until about the 1960s. In 1967, Winn's started trading in Belmont, Cessnock and Cardiff in the hope of trying to keep afloat at a time when modern department stores were proving more attractive than old-fashioned family drapery businesses.

Winn's was very generous to family members purchasing goods at the various stores. There were a lot of us and we only had to pay cost price plus 5 per cent, which would have eaten into profits. Winn's also employed four generations of the family, including myself which probably was not a recipe for success in turbulent trading times.

During the late 1960s, I worked at the emporium at 16–30 Oxford Street each December school holidays in the lead-up to Christmas. By this time, Winn's sold everything department stores like David Jones sold, including kitchenware and clothes, but it was rather down-market and old-fashioned, and, instead of modern tills, it continued to use a vacuum tube system to issue customer change and receipts.

I usually worked in the corsetry section and had to stand on my feet all day, even though there were few customers. My job was to measure old ladies in the change room and assist them to lace the back of the new corsets for size. I also helped them select their favoured slinky salmon pink underpants in sizes so vast they were unimaginable to a schoolgirl. Once, when the World War 2 amputee employee who regularly manned the lift was absent, I was allowed to take his place, which meant that I was out of sight much of the time and could sit on the lift stool – a dream job.

Most family members had shares in the company. My mother Helen, who wasn't really even a Winn, and I held onto our shares out of loyalty even though it was clear Winn's would not survive. Of course, by the end, our shares were worthless, while other more canny, less sentimental family shareholders wisely sold out in time to salvage something.

Winn's went into voluntary liquidation in 1978 and ceased operations in Newcastle on 19 January 1980 after 101 years in the city. The Sydney business struggled on, selling the Oxford Street premises and moving its headquarters to 199 Regent Street, Redfern in 1973. It finally went into receivership in 1982.

Acknowledgements

More than a decade ago, I conducted a series of videotaped interviews with Roy's sons Dick and Murray Winn, their wives Helen and Evelyne, and their first cousin Janet Winn. I wanted to draw out their memories of Roy and the world in which he lived. I especially wanted to understand this man who had been such a pioneering psychoanalyst in Australia and had been held in high esteem by my father, but who had been a slightly forbidding figure to me. Regrettably, none of my interviewees are alive to see the results. Nevertheless, I am enormously grateful to them for providing the material that helped to frame this biography.

Roy's daughter, Betty Ferguson, died before I had come up with the idea for this book, so I am without her considerable talents. Betty was an accomplished amateur historian who had researched the Winn history and found the family seat at Nostell Priory[377] in West Yorkshire. As Roy's oldest child, I am sure Betty would have had much to say about her father that will now regrettably remain unsaid. Still, I owe her a considerable debt, as I became the beneficiary of her efforts to assemble a repository of biographical material on Roy.

Betty's children, Robert Ferguson and Cathy Jarratt, who often visited Roy from school and knew him longer than I did, have provided letters, photos, diaries and numerous anecdotes of Roy's later years. My brother, Roger Winn, emailed his childhood memories of both Roy

---

377 See Appendix 2. William Winn and Winn's Ltd history

Winn cousins: Daniel, Cathy, Margaret, Pru in front, Dominique, Roger, Robert

and the Fairy Bower house. Murray's children, Daniel and Dominique Winn, too young to have remembered much, found an invaluable stash of papers and photos. Dominique's daughter, Nina Meehan, cleverly photoshopped an important photograph. My second cousin, Pru Brewer, joined me in the search for the McMurtrie house at Point Piper and bequeathed me a cache of letters that Roy had written to her great aunt, Ellie McMurtrie.

While my own Winn family provided me with invaluable hard copy, my partner, Andrew Dix and my sisters-in-law, Jane Dix and Louise Dix, assisted with geographical exploration of Winn sites in Australia and Europe. Andrew, always bemused by, but ever-supportive of my eclectic projects, helped me track down Roy's movements in First World War France and Belgium, and Jane's fluent French enabled us to discover both Kandahar Farm, where Roy was taken after being wounded at Messines, and the Bailleul hospital where his foot was amputated. Louise found archival photographs of Winn's Ltd premises, and lead a sleuthing expedition to find and record the three main Winn houses in Mayfield, Newcastle.

Richard Travers, a lawyer and artist who has written his own books on the First World War, fact-checked the war section of the biography and pointed the way to additional archival materials.

Psychoanalysts Maria Teresa Hooke and Leonie Sullivan did the same for the psychoanalytical chapters. They directed me to useful contacts, but most importantly, helped me to understand the various schools and trends within the psychoanalytical profession. The psychoanalytic psychotherapist Christine Brett Vickers provided additional information about the establishment of the psychoanalytical institutes in Melbourne and Sydney.

Andrew's former secretary, Marianne Lee, typed Roy's autobiographical novel *Men May Rise*, so that I had a digital version for distribution. Journalist and editor Shelley Gare edited the typescript and asked penetrating questions that helped reveal new insights into Roy's story. Publisher John Kerr was, thankfully, beautifully professional and uncompromisingly frank, and designer Paul Taylder cared as much about the book's aesthetics as I did about the text. My thanks to all.

Indexes

General Index

A Mebb/ A. Meeb (*pseudonym*) 133–134
Abbeville 45
Abingdon 71
Albert 49, 55
Adler, Alfred 104, 105
Alexander, Franz 104, 108
Alexandria 36
Alexandria Quartet 114
Amiens 45, 55
Amoeba 132, 133, 135, 147
Amoeba (*poem*) 134
Angevin 45
Angus & Robertson 139
Anzac Cove 21–35
Anzac Medical Association 29
Are Allusive Sequences "Symbolic"? 107
Aristotle 135
Armistice 78–79
Arnott, Mabel 113
Arnott, William 9
Ascham School 126
Australia House 98
Australian Association of Psychology & Philosophy 94
Australian Medical Association 103
Australian Medical Congress 81
Australian Medical Corps 19
Australian Psychoanalytical Society 102
Australian Psychological Centre 99
Australian Seashores 127

Bacon, Francis 109
Bader, Canon 112
Bahai Temple, Terrey Hills 112
Bailleul 45, 68–69, 70
Bapaume 49, 60
Bazentin Ridge 48, 58

Bean, Charles 63
Begg, Colonel 30
Binet, Albert 94
Birdwood, General 57
Birkenhead, Violet 123
Bondi Baths 118
Borderline Concept 106
Boulogne 69
Bowker, Binkie 118
Boy Scouts 93
Braeside 11
Brewer, Pru 11
Brill, Abraham 102
British and Foreign Bible Society 10
British Psychoanalytical Society 84, 95, 98–100, 102
Browne, Betty 63, 73–75 (*see* Winn, Bertha)
Browne, Phillip 74
Buckingham Palace 72
Bullecourt 60–63

Cairo 18, 20–22
Cameron, Donald 10
Cameron, Sophia 10
Cannibalism (*poem*) 120
Cape Helles 21
Casino de Paris 21
Castle, The 123–126, 143
Challenges to Mental Combat & Crackpottery 120, 131–135
Church Missionary Society 41
Coast Hospital 89
Concord Veteran's Repatriation Hospital 141
'Contributions of Psycho-Analysis to General Medicine' 103

Copsley 71–75
Cox, Maj Gen Sir H V 71
Cranbrook School 117, 118, 126
Crickmore, Clara 74
'Cultivating Optimism' 109

Dakin, John 127
Damousi, Joy 91, 98, 100
Dane, Paul 92, 98–99
Derrie (*dog*) 111
Dickebusch 55–56
Dickens, Charles 109
Diploma of Psychological Medicine 83
Dover 70
Durrell, Lawrence 114

Egypt (*poem*) 42
Egypt 19–22, 35–42, 125, 132
Einstein 135
Ellingsen, Peter 91, 98, 100
Ellis, Havelock 81
English Hospital, Wimereux 69
Evolution (*poem*) 133
Exeter Hospital 70

Fairy Bower 123, 127, 141–142
Felton, Ken 118
Ferenczi, Sandor 95
Ferguson, Alan 122
Ferguson, Betty (*see* Winn, Betty)
Ferguson, Gordon 119, 122–123
Ferguson, Robert 125–126, 128–129
Fink, Dr Siegfried 99–100
1st Light Horse Field Ambulance 24, 30
Fisherman's Hut 24–27
Flers 58
Flugel, John 102
14th Australian Infantry Battalion 27, 46–47, 48–49, 53, 55, 58–9
4th Australian Division 46–47, 52, 60, 63, 67, 71–72

4th Australian Brigade 27–28, 36, 46, 60–61, 63–64
4th Field Ambulance 31, 44, 59, 60, 64, 72
Freemasons Lodge of Sydney University 116
Freud, Sigmund 80–81, 91, 94–7, 102–105, 145

Gale, Walter 123
Gallipoli 3, 4, 22–37, 42, 57
Galton, Francis 94
Gelibolu 21
Gellife, Dr Ely 90
George V, King 72–73
Goolwa 87
Graham, Frank 143–145
Great Depression 92, 121

Haig, Field Marshal Douglas 72
Hamlet 40
Harley Building 91, 93
Hay Valley 30
Heliopolis Palace Hotel 19
Hindenburg Line 60–61
Homer 14, 90
Hurford, Ellen (Nanny) 2, 87, 113, 121, 127
Hylands Hotel 118

I am a Man (*poem*) 146–147
Imbros 29
International Psychoanalytical Society 93, 98, 102
Interpretation of Dreams 97
'Interrelationships between the Development of Speech & Locomotion' 95
Ismailia 36

Jacka, Lt Albert 57
Jarratt, Cathy *née* Ferguson 126–127

Jimmie (*dog*) 111
Jones, Ernest 81, 84, 86, 93, 98–9, 102, 145
Joseph, Betty 95–96
Joy (*fictional*) 75
Jung, Carl 81, 104

Kamsur (*Egyptian wind*) 38
Kandahar Farm 68–69
Kitchener, Field Marshal Lord 33, 41
Klein, Melanie 93, 95, 102–03, 107, 144
Knee, Mr 113
Korea 102
Kosciusko, Hotel 120

Lacan, Jacques 95
Lady Martins Beach 11
Lake Conjola 118
Lazar-Geroe, Dr Clara 99–100, 102
Lemnos 22, 27
Lincolnshire 7
List of Slips in Diagnosis (*poem*) 90
London Institute of Psychoanalysis 100
Long Bacon (*short story*) 108
Loughran, Henry 27
Lyons 45
Lyric Theatre 59

Mackay, Sir Iven 117
Malinowski, Bronislaw 84
Manly Musical Society 142
Marseilles 45
Martin, Reg 92, 100, 144
Matador (*dog*) 127–128
Maudsley Neurological Hospital 83, 90
McDougall, Dr William 90
McMurtrie, Helen (*see* Winn, Ellie)
McMurtrie, Ida (*see* Winn, Ida)
Mead, Margaret 94
Meals on Wheels 142
Medical Journal of Australia 92, 101, 103, 143

Medical Re-survey Board 83
Melbourne Institute of Psychoanalysis 99, 106, 107
Men May Rise 3, 16, 53, 73, 120, 131
'Mental Development' 95, 106
Meredith, George 109
Messines 63–64, 67, 69, 72
Methodist Church 9–10, 14–15, 30, 59
Methodist Foreign Missionary Society 10
Military Cross 72
Ministry of Pensions 83
Monash, Maj Gen John 63
Monty (*dog*) 111
Monty (*shark*) 119–120
Mott, Sir Frederick 90
Mouquet Farm 48–55
Mudros 22, 27, 35
My Ideography 109, 131–133

Nanny (*see* Hurford)
Neuve Eglise 64, 68
NSW Institution for the Deaf, Dumb and Blind 11
NSW Temperance Alliance 9
New Theatre 63
Newington College 14–15
Newton, Isaac 135
Newtown Baby Health Centre 89
Nield, Janet 100, 108–109, 143–144
971 (*hill at Gallipoli*) 28
Noreuil 61
North Middlesex Hospital 83
Northern Suburbs Crematorium 141
Northumberland House 84
No 1 Australian General Hospital 19
No 1 Australian CCS 69
No 2 Australian CCS 68

Odyssey 14
Oedipus 107
Old Lady Shows her Medals 63

Orontes SS 19
Otago Gully 30

Pagan, Jock 112
Palestine 36
Parkes, Cobden 2
Parkes, Eleanor 2
Parkes, Sir Henry 2
Pavlov, Ivan 94–95, 104, 108
Peggy 73, 79
Peggy the Second 73
Peggy the Third 79
Peto, Dr Andrew 100–102
Port Hacking 77–78
Poseidon 29
Pozières 48–55, 57, 68
Pratt, Frank 38
Prince of Wales 38
'Psychoanalysis and Allied Forms of Therapy' 103–105
'Psychoanalysis and General Practice' 103
'Psychoanalysis and other Forms of Psychotherapy' 103–105
'Psychoanalysis in War-Time' 106
Push, The 47–48

Red Cross 71
Red Sea 37
Riggall, Dr R M 84–86, 98–99
Rockley 12–14, 78
Roheim, Geza 102
Rookwood 10, 122
Roy Winn Library 102
Royal Australian Historical Society 94
Royal Prince Alfred Hospital 17, 19
Royal Sydney Golf Club 116

St Catherine's School 123
St Mark's Anglican Church 112–123
St Michael's Anglican Church 111
Salvation Army 10
Samothrace 29

Sausage Gully 49
Savoy Theatre 59
Scheherazade 135–136
Selton, Tas (*fictional*) 3
Serapeum 36–39, 41
Shade, Janet (*see* Winn, Janet)
Shade, Thomas 10
Shakespeare 40, 108
Shark Is 79
Sheik-el-Beled 21
Sinclair MacLagan, Maj Gen 72
60 (*hill*) 55
Somme Offensive 47–48, 57
Song, A (*poem*) 111, 125
Sophocles 107
Spanish Influenza Epidemic 80
Stewart, Dr Grainge 90
Stony Trench 58
Stroud 10
Suez Canal 36–37
Sujester (*pseudonym*) 134–136
Sydney Camp 58
Sydney Grammar School 14–15
Sydney Hospital 80–83, 89–90, 92–3
Sydney Institute for Psychoanalysis 100–102
Sydney University (*see* University of Sydney)
Syme amputation 69

Taiwan 102
Tel El Kebir 36
3rd Australian Division 63
3rd London General Hospital 70
Timon of Athens 108
'*Timon of Athens* and Rorschach Tests' 108
Toynbee, Arnold 135
Trobriand Islands 84
Trojan War 29
Truscott, John (*pseudonym*) 3

United Grand Lodge of NSW 116
University College, London 83
University of Sydney 16–17, 116, 127–129

Victoria Cross 36, 57

Walden Grove 30–32
Weeroona 117–118
Wesley Chapel, City Road 59
Wesley, John 59
Wesleyan Mission Hall 59
West London Hospital 83
White, Patrick 114
Wimereux 69
Windmill, The 49
Winn Clinic 102
Winn Court 7
Winn Hall 9
Winn, Annesley 12
Winn, Bertha *née* Browne 2, 5, 63, 73–75, 77–80, 83, 85–86, 93, 110–122, 145
Winn, Betty 5, 14, 83, 87, 110–116, 118–119, 123
Winn, Edena 12
Winn, Ellie *née* McMurtie 5, 9, 11, 38, 40, 42, 60, 113
Winn, Evelyne *née* Gey 2, 126–127, 129, 143, 145
Winn, Gordon Russell 9, 11, 14–15, 38, 113, 115
Winn, Harold 5, 9, 11, 12, 14–15, 38, 111, 115, 118
Winn, Harriet *née* Coupland 7, 10, 122
Winn, Harry 12
Winn, Helen *née* Parkes 2, 126–127, 143
Winn, Henrietta (Isabel) *née* Arrell 12
Winn, Ida *née* McMurtie 11, 38, 113
Winn, Isaac 8, 12
Winn, Janet *née* Shade 7–12, 15–16, 113

Winn, Janet (*daughter of Harold*) 2, 11, 14, 113, 118
Winn, Jessie Harriet 12
Winn, John 7
Winn, Murray 2, 3, 13–14, 110–111, 113–114, 116–117, 120–123, 128–129, 141, 143, 145
Winn, Nell *née* Gale 2, 123–129, 142–143
Winn, Nora 11, 113
Winn, Reta 12
Winn, Richard William (Dick) 1, 2, 3, 5, 12–15, 27, 83, 86–87, 92–93, 100, 110, 111, 113–123, 126–127, 141, 143, 146
Winn, Rodney 12
Winn, Roger 120, 126–127
Winn, Stanley Dickson 11
Winn, Stanley (*son of Stanley Dickson*), 12
Winn, William (Wowser) 7–15, 70, 78, 113, 121–122, 145
Winn, William Harold (*see* Winn, Harold)
Winn's Ltd 7–8, 10–12, 70, 92, 121, 142
Winnonaville 7
Women's Legion 71

Young Men's Christian Association 115
Ypres 63–64

Zouaves 58

Index to Appendix 2

Adam, Robert 151
Aird, John Cameron 155
Aird, Mary Ann (Marian) *née* Shade 155
Allworth Park 154
Annesley House 157
Argyllshire 154
Arnott Holme 157
Australian Agricultural Co 152
Australian Imperial Force Ambulance Fund 163

Balmain 160
Belfast 160
Belmont 164
Bradford 159
Brewer, Pru 154
Brilliant 154

Cameron, Anne *née* McPherson 153
Cameron, Donald 153
Cameron, Sophia 153
Camperdown 161
Cardiff NSW 164
Carlton 155
Cessnock 164
Chippendale 151
Clarke, Harriet (*see* Winn, Harriet) 153
Coupland's Eradica 153

Elizabeth I 151

Factory Lunatic Asylum 152
Ferguson, Betty *née* Winn 152, 155
Ferguson, Gordon 155

Glasgow 160
Great Depression 162
Griffiths, Anne 162
Gwydir 151

Harrison, John 151
Henry VIII 151

Japan 161
Just for Fun 163

Kittson, Maria *née* Winn 152

Leichhardt 160
Lincolnshire 151–152
London 159
Long, Sydney 159

Manchester 160
Mayfield Ridge 157–158
Melbourne 155, 158–159
National Trust 152

NSW Institution for the Deaf... 154
Newcastle 154, 155, 157–164
Niagara 160
North Sydney 160
Nostell Priory 151–152

Oxford Street 161

Parkes, Helen (*see* Winn, Helen)

Redfern 154, 161, 164
Rockley 158
Rookwood 153

St Andrew's Church 153
St Peter's Church Hamilton 152–153
Shade, Sophia *née* Cameron 153
Shade, Thomas 153
Streeton, Arthur 159

Templar 152

W Winn & Co 159
Wales 151
Waterhole Reach Farm 154
Weeroona 159
Winn Court 157–158
Winn, Anne *née* Webb 152
Winn, Annesley 155
Winn, Bertha *née* Browne 155
Winn, Betty *née* Ferguson 155
Winn, Catherine *née* Rutledge 152
Winn, Edena 155
Winn, Euphemia (Effie) *née* Arnott 152, 157
Winn, Evelyne *née* Gey 155
Winn, Gordon Russell 154, 160
Winn, Harold 154, 157, 159–160
Winn, Harriet *née* Coupland 152-3, 155, 160
Winn, Harry 155
Winn, Helen (Ellie) *née* McMurtrie 154
Winn, Helen *née* Parkes 155, 164
Winn, Ida *née* McMurtrie 154
Winn, Isaac 152, 155, 157, 159, 161–162
Winn, Henrietta (Isabel) *née* Arrell 154–155
Winn, Janet (Jessie) *née* Shade 153–155
Winn, Janet (*daughter of Harold*) 154, 159
Winn, Jessie Harriet 155
Winn, John (a.k.a. Isaac & James) 152
Winn, Murray 155
Winn, Nora 154
Winn, Reta 155
Winn, Richard (Dick) 155
Winn, Robert 152, 155
Winn, Rodney 155
Winn, Roy 153, 155
Winn, Sir George 151
Winn, Sir Rowland 151
Winn, Stanley Dickinson 154–155
Winn, William (1849–1929) 152–155, 158–63
Winn, William Harold (Harold) (*see* Winn, Harold)
Winn, William (*son of Isaac*) 161
Winn & Co 155
Winn's Ltd 154, 159, 161–164
Winn's Ltd 50th Jubilee 163
Winn's stores 150, 152–153
Winn's Thrift Club 163
Winnahra house 157
Winnetta sewing machine 161
Winnonaville 156, 157
Wynne, George 151

Yorkshire 151

www.ingramcontent.com/pod-product-compliance
Lightning Source LLC
Chambersburg PA
CBHW042140160426
43201CB00021B/2346